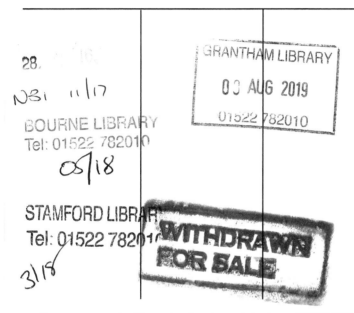

Political Correctness and the Destruction of Social Order

Howard S. Schwartz

Political Correctness and the Destruction of Social Order

Chronicling the Rise of the Pristine Self

Howard S. Schwartz
Oakland University
Jackson Heights, New York, USA

ISBN 978-3-319-39804-4 ISBN 978-3-319-39805-1 (eBook)
DOI 10.1007/978-3-319-39805-1

Library of Congress Control Number: 2016947970

Printed on acid-free paper

This Palgrave Macmillan imprint is published by Springer Nature
The registered company is Springer International Publishing AG Switzerland

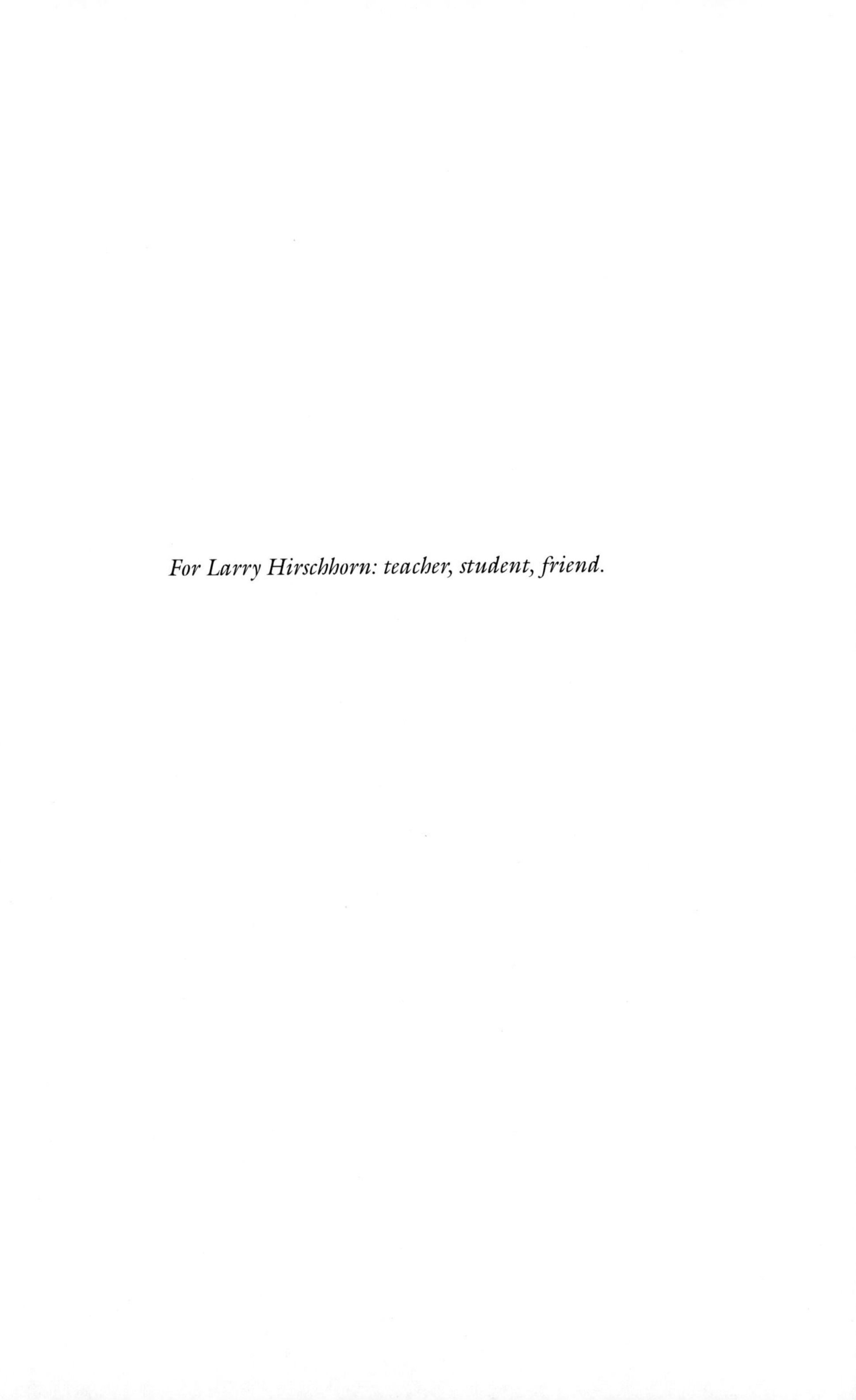

For Larry Hirschhorn: teacher, student, friend.

Trigger Warning

Lasciate ogni speranza, voi ch'entrate!

—Dante Alighieri

Acknowledgments

A number of people have read parts of this manuscript and have given me the benefit of their wise counsel. Among them are Larry Hirschhorn, James Knoll, Jim Krantz, Thomas Hoffman, Brigid Nossal, Halina Brunning, Simon Western, David Armstrong, Philip Boxer, Stanley Gold, and, as always, Ann Winston. I'd like to thank them all and also the International Society for the Psychoanalytic Study of Organizations, of which most are members, for providing me intellectual companionship and a venue for presenting my work.

I would also like to thank my colleagues at the School of Business Administration (SBA) at Oakland University (OU), from which I recently retired. The work that I do can easily lead a scholar to find himself in extreme tension with his academic milieu. That never happened to me at Oakland. I believe that my colleagues were, for the most part, about as liberal as in almost any American university, but they never thought to interfere with the work I was doing. I think there were a number of reasons for that, but one of them was, ironically, our diversity.

That diversity was really quite a wonder. My colleagues came from almost everywhere. Offhand, I can think of India, China, Nigeria, Iran, Korea, Australia, Israel, Eastern Europe, and Jamaica; and there were several African-Americans, not to mention some of us native white Americans, like me. But that just happened. We were never fashionable in our hiring practices. We just, as my colleague John Henke once put it, hired the best people we could and diversity took care of itself. But with that many cultures, and readers should keep this in mind when they read Chap. 3, there was less likelihood that the hothouse monoculture that has afflicted so much of American academia could become dominant, and it did not.

Of course, hiring people based on their qualifications was the old way of doing things. We never saw ourselves as moving to the forefront of political change, and were content to do our work well, in the way that academic work has always been defined. And when we hired people, we were attracted to those we thought would define their jobs in the same way. There was nothing in that way that was consistent with the political correctness that, like an invasive species, took over so many other places. You can call it anything you like. I call it being conservative.

The irony is that the wreckage that identity politics has wrought through much of American academia, and which has been most pronounced at the higher levels of the prestige hierarchy, never touched us, and the result, I believe, is that the quality of the education we delivered, and of the research we did, would have increased our relative ranking quite considerably on any objective measure of quality, if anybody kept track of these things and knew we were there.

But we knew. And I can tell you that if you are looking for a good place to send your kids to college, you could do much worse than the SBA at OU.

Contents

List of Figures

CHAPTER 1

Introduction: The Hedgehog is Embarrassed by his Riches

The fox, Isaiah Berlin, famously said, knows many things. The hedgehog, by contrast, knows only one important thing. But, of course, whether the thing that the hedgehog knows is really important is not something the hedgehog, whose bias in this matter defines his life, can, with any objective authority, say.

And so when it happens, after several decades, that life simply erupts with instance after instance that validate his obsession, and whose importance nobody even thinks to deny, the hedgehog may find himself gratified, but may also come into possession of a range of emotions that are unfamiliar and, however pleasing, more than a little bit weird.

This is my third book on the psychological processes underlying political correctness. For the previous two books, when it came time, after the substantive work had been done, to write the introduction, I looked for contemporary illustrative events and ideas that would attract the reader's attention. There was always something, and I had no doubt that there always would be. But what I am finding now is that, far from there being an issue of finding something, there is a problem of sorting my way through *everything*, and this stuff *already* has readers' attention. Something new happens every day and every one of them is fascinating enough to qualify for a place in my introduction. The question of selection, then, is no longer one of weighing the virtues of various candidates, but of arbitrarily picking a date, selecting the current outrage, and resolving to stick with

H.S. Schwartz, *Political Correctness and the Destruction of Social Order*, DOI 10.1007/978-3-319-39805-1_1

it, as a way of moving on to the other matters that need my attention in finishing the book.

The point is that political correctness is everywhere, and even liberal publications like *The New York Times* and *The Atlantic*, that previously ignored such matters, are now beginning to give them serious attention. For example, in running up to Halloween, which is tomorrow, *The Times* devoted a 1500-word article to the way college campuses, on the lookout for the brand-new crime of "cultural appropriation," have been dictating what can and cannot be worn. (Johnson 2015). Summing up:

> As colleges debate the lines between cultural sensitivity and free speech, they are issuing recommendations for Halloween costumes on campus, aimed at fending off even a hint of offense in students' choice of attire. Using the fairly new yardstick of cultural appropriation—which means pretending for fun or profit to be a member of an ethnic, racial or gender group to which you do not belong—schools, student groups and fraternity associations are sending a message that can be summed up in five words: It is dangerous to pretend.

For me, what is particularly gratifying, and even new, is the way the commenters on these articles, almost unanimously, find these developments absurd and even outrageous. One representative view was from "Peter," who gained 263 recommendations for writing that

> So people can't dress up as a mariachi band, even though mariachi bands exist and members of mariachi bands often wear sombreros and ponchos? Can a person dress up as a cop or a nurse if they aren't actually cops or nurses? Are Americans not allowed to wear Dia de los Muertos-style facepaint and outfits because they originated in Mexico? Are Mexicans not allowed to participate in American Halloween parties dressed as Marty McFly?
>
> I consider myself pretty culturally sensitive, but this is cultural hypersensitivity run amok. It's Halloween—for one night a year you just dress up like someone you're not. It's that simple.

But the point I want to emphasize was summed up by "Manhattan William" who said: "People are losing their minds."

People are indeed losing their minds, I aver, but the sign of this is not primarily the apparently exponential growth of examples; that could just be the fashion. It is the fact that the nature of the examples themselves seems to represent a shift of the whole society toward the fringes of madness.

When I say madness I am not just talking about garden-variety neurosis. There has never been any shortage of that, and it has not been entirely unsalutary. I am talking about something else, and there is no better index of it than what I call the level of ambient rage. Rage is different from anger. Anger is directed, and bounded. Rage is diffuse and unbounded. If it seems to have a focus at one point, it can have an entirely different one at the next. Most importantly, it has become impossible to predict what will set people off. Who would have thought, for example, that the idea of Halloween costumes would occasion such fury?

In this book, I am going to try to gain some understanding of this madness though the use of psychoanalytic theory, but first a little bit of physics may be useful in providing an analogy.

Everybody knows that energy is to be had from the transformation of matter at the level of atoms and molecules. That's chemical energy, and of course we see it whenever we drink a cup of coffee or start our car. But we also know that a quite different level of energy is brought out when an atomic bomb is set off. That's nuclear energy.

Nuclear energy is released when the nuclei of atoms are split and the energy that previously held the nuclei together is unbound. Of course, the amount of energy in a single atomic nucleus is not much, but there are many atoms and when you release the energy holding together a zillion of them, you get quite a bang.

That's where we are today, except what is being split is not atomic nuclei but human minds. So when we say that people are losing their minds, we really mean it.

The occasion for this has been what I call the rise, or the establishment, or the normalization, of the pristine self. This is a self that is touched by nothing but love. The problem is that nobody is touched by nothing but love, and so if a person has this as an expectation, if they have built their sense of themselves around this premise, the inevitable appearance of something other than love, indeed the appearance even of any other human being, blows this structure apart. That is where we are today.

Where the idea of the pristine self has come from, how it and its decomposition have become manifest, and what the effects of this are likely to be, are the subjects of this book. I cannot offer a happy prognosis here, except to say that nothing lasts forever. This, too, shall pass and when it does those who are left will need to know how what happened to them happened. So I am writing a chronicle now. Hopefully, when the time comes, it will be of use.

This is a work of what I call psychoanalytic phenomenology. My subject matter is my own mind. I try to understand the minds of others by finding them within my own. As I have said, my theoretical framework for this is psychoanalytic, and that calls for a word of explanation. The credibility of psychoanalytic theory is, of course, not universally granted. It has, however, a unique suitability to the study of political correctness. There is clearly an element of irrationality in political correctness. It is a form of censorship without a censor; we impose it on ourselves. Yet, it keeps us away from the reasoned discussion of social issues which everybody can see are important, consequential, and desperately in need of wide-ranging analysis. It does so through an emotional power that is rarely gainsaid and which anyone can see is ultimately against everyone's interest; yet it prevails nonetheless. If that is not irrationality playing itself out in the social domain, what is?

Yet where does it get that power? This is a question that is rarely posed—it is, after all, politically incorrect to do so—but it is no less important than the totality of the issues that political correctness has obscured. And if we do not approach this question through psychoanalytic theory, what, exactly, shall we approach it through? The rational understanding of irrationality is what psychoanalysis was developed to accomplish. In fact, more than any specific theory that is what psychoanalysis is. It is in that spirit that we will undertake this inquiry.

—Jackson Heights, New York

Reference

Johnson, Kirk. 2015. Halloween Costume Correctness on Campus: Feel Free to Be You, but Not Me. *New York Times*, October 30.

CHAPTER 2

The Pristine Self: Psychodynamics of the Anti-Bullying Movement

The anti-bullying movement came upon us like a summer storm. All of a sudden, everywhere was the belief that bullying is everywhere, and that it is intolerable. Schools all over the place were moved to stamp it out. The US President got out in front of this by calling a White House Conference. Under enormous pressure, and with the highest sense of urgency, laws were proposed and passed in 49 states (Clark 2013). To be sure, there is somewhat less publicity now, in 2015, than there was a couple of years ago, but that probably just means that the movement has become institutionalized. Certainly there can be no doubt about its social power.

But where has this power come from? There is no reason to believe that it was generated as a response to an increase in the incidence of bullying. There is no evidence of that, and in fact what evidence is there seems to indicate that the level of bullying has declined over the last two decades.

Writing in a publication of the Crimes Against Children Research Center of the University of New Hampshire, David Finkelhor (2013), summarized the findings from youth surveys that had tracked bullying and related phenomena.[1] His conclusion:

> The surveys that reflect change over the longest time periods, going back to the early 1990s, consistently show declines in bullying and peer victimization, some of it remarkably large. The more recent trends, since 2007, show some declines, but less consistently.

H.S. Schwartz, *Political Correctness and the Destruction of Social Order*, DOI 10.1007/978-3-319-39805-1_2

This suggests that the interesting question is not so much what to do about bullying, but about how the idea developed that bullying is everywhere, and that it therefore is a phenomenon that something needs to be done about.

In what follows, I am going to try to make sense of the movement against bullying. In doing this, I will make the assumption that this movement is of a piece; that whether the focal points are workplace bullying, or school bullying, these various concerns are driven by the same dynamics. I think this is a reasonable assumption, given that they all arose at the same time and have the same general orientation.

For purposes of theory development, however, I will look at only one area of the anti-bullying movement, which is the concern with school bullying. This idea invokes the image of damage to children, and this is where I believe its emotional center is located, and where it derives its power.

Looking at the matter this way presents us with an interesting paradox, which is that school bullying, in practice, encompasses individuals who, in previous times, would not have been considered children at all. For example, a *New York Times* article on the relationship between bullying and suicide, focusing on the case of Rutgers University student Tyler Clementi, relies on a study of "students between the ages of 11 and 22" (Schwartz, J 2010).

I submit that it is the treatment of people well into their twenties as children that provides us with our first clue about the nature of the dynamics in question. The anti-bullying movement treats people as children, whether they are, in any realistic sense, or not. It does not seek to limit its efforts to those areas most central to its concerns, but rather expands to areas outside of its focal point and bring its concerns along with it.

I will try to show that this would tend to perpetuate childhood and establish it as the normal way of living life. The corollary of this would be the diminution of adulthood.

Looking at the matter this way suggests that the anti-bullying movement is not actually about bullying, but about something much broader; and that the way to understand it is to get at the broader phenomenon of which it is part.

My claim is that the anti-bullying movement is an avatar of political correctness; one of a range of social processes that go under that label. It is, moreover, an avatar of a very particular sort. Political correctness, by itself is, a very controversial matter. It has its power, but that power is often contested. Almost anyone, for example, will acknowledge the category of things representing political correctness run amuck. Being against bullying is not ordinarily subject to that kind of check. To the extent that it arises from, and brings with it, the kind of dangerous dynamics which almost anyone will be able to associate with political correctness, it can do so in a way that is very difficult to oppose. If it is an avatar, it is an avatar of a very dangerous sort.

As I have said, it aims to protect children, but it also reinforces childhood and establishes it as the normal way of living life, at the expense of adulthood. But there is a powerful irony at work here. Bullying is a perfectly normal way for children to relate to one another. The cure for it is growing up. Adulthood is the only way that bullying can be recognized as bullying, and thereby gotten over. The result is that the logic of the anti-bullying movement leads to a condition in which bullying is not eliminated, but, through the prolongation of childhood, made universal.

The Pristine Self

The key to my analysis is the proposition that the anti-bullying movement offers as normal what I will call *the pristine self*. The pristine self is an idea of the self as not having a boundary around it; it is not thought to need one.[2] A person necessarily encounters other persons, but in the model of the pristine self such experiences with others are exclusively a matter of being loved. We form a boundary when we need to defend ourselves against the negative feelings that others have toward us. In an interpersonal universe made out of love for us, such boundaries would not develop. But while this universe of love sounds appealing, and certainly the idea that we can hold ourselves entirely open to the feelings of others sounds appealing, such appeals are superficial. The boundaryless, pristine self, properly understood, poses dangers to society that are very serious, and ultimately these are what I would like to bring to our attention.

My plan will be to first explain the psychological underpinnings of political correctness, then to show that the anti-bullying movement expresses that psychology and how political correctness and the anti-bullying movement establish as normal the boundaryless, pristine self. Then, I want to show the negative consequences of all this for social organization. Finally, I will illustrate some of these points through analysis of a case of bullying and anti-bullying in the USA.

Oedipal and Anti-Oedipal Psychology

As I have said, the key to understanding the anti-bullying movement is political correctness, and the key to understanding political correctness is what I have called anti-Oedipal psychology (Schwartz 2010). But the best way to understand anti-Oedipal psychology is to understand the Oedipal psychology that it is defined against. That is a relatively easy matter, because it is based on a story that will be familiar to many, Freud's adaptation of the myth of Oedipus, which here will be slightly adumbrated for our use.

Freud tells us that, in the beginning of psychological life, we do not experience ourselves as separate from mother, but as fused with her. In this state, life is perfect. Mother is the world to us and loves us entirely. We thus experience ourselves as the center of a loving world, a condition Freud refers to as primary narcissism, and whose appeal is obvious. The advent of any degree of separation has the result that we desire to return to it. Mother, then, is the unique object of our desire. We want to marry her, as Oedipus did.

The problem is that father stands in the way. He has a bond with mother that does not revolve around us. We must get him out of our way, kill him, so we can marry and fuse with mother again. But there is a problem. Father is big and we are small. If a fight develops between us and father, it is not we who will kill him, but he who will kill us. In fact, he does not even have to kill us. He can cut off our penis, such as it is, and end the rivalry that way. The result is pure terror on our part, with the fear of being castrated being ever present.[3]

What a quandary we are in! What shall we do? Well, it is not inevitable that we do anything. Some people spend their whole lives in a condition of castration anxiety, afraid that if they follow their desires they will be mutilated by authority. But luckily, for most of us, there is another way. We can become like father, and then we will be able to have, not mother exactly, but someone like mother. More precisely, we will be able to have a bond with mother, as father has, and which we understand in the only way we can, as the kind of close loving embrace that we remember from our early experience. This program of becoming like father proceeds first through identification and then through the internalization of father's way of approaching the world, so that we can thrive in it as father has, gaining love through accomplishments in the world as father has gained love.

It is this pursuit of mother's love, unconscious though it may be, that provides us with the motivation to do what we must do in the world to fulfill the obligations that come to us as adults, such as the necessity to make a living through work. In this way, through our efforts, the world is constructed. That, taken all together, is what I call Oedipal psychology.

But notice here that all this is based on the idea that mother and father are bonded in a way that we would like to have. Mother, that is to say, loves father. But what if she does not?

Why should she?

As we saw before, the child's love for mother is absolute, and is based on her love for the child. For the child, that love, by itself, is enough to make life perfect. This must impart to the child's image of mother, which we may call the maternal imago, a degree of benevolence and omnipotence that nothing in real life can ever match, nor to which anything can even come close.[4]

Look at this from the other side. The infant's image of mother, the maternal imago, is an image that mother can have of herself. As Lacan observes, the image we have of ourselves is always a misrepresentation. In the nature of things, we cannot get it right. The only question is in what way do we get it wrong. This way is spectacular.

Seeing herself as the infant sees her, mother would be the fount of all goodness in the world. She would be omnipotent. Her love would make anyone feel perfectly loved and would be all anyone could need. Her very presence would make life perfect. After all, as John Lennon wrote, all you need is love, right?

Set against the prodigies she could perform, what would there be about a man's accomplishments that could possibly register as being worthwhile. Even the best would be compromised, partial, and imperfect. Indeed, by acting in the world, creating a world that reflects him and is organized around his needs, he has taken away the possibility of her creating a far better world just by being herself.

Given her importance, it must be that the whole world that he has created is organized around her; not to please her, as it is in the Oedipal model, but to subordinate and repress her. Organization, as he has created it, is nothing but organized oppression. On what basis could he possibly claim a right to her affections? In these circumstances, her attitude toward him would not be one of love, but of contempt, hatred, and resentment.

How would this impact the child? Just as the child in the Oedipal model takes its cue from the mother's love for the father, so in this case it would take its cue from her hatred and resentment. This is the basis of anti-Oedipal psychology.

Obviously, this would undercut his reason for admiring the father and wanting to become like him. The father has not earned mother's love through his accomplishments, but has stolen it from the child. This turns the psychological basis of life upside down. Instead of wanting to become like the father, the child would want to get rid of the father, in that way returning to the mother's love by removing the barrier that stands in the way.

Later on, I will show that the attack upon the father in the name of the omnipotent, primordial mother is the core of political correctness.

For our present purposes, the crucial matter is the transformation in the child's conception of himself. In Oedipal psychology, the child sees himself as a child, as not yet an adult. It would see adulthood, gained through accomplishment in an indifferent world, as the proper model for its development, as a potentiality that it must actualize. It is what the child is to become, though it is not there yet. Identity as an adult is the person's real identity, even though it must be created through work which one has not done yet.

In anti-Oedipal psychology, the model of the adult as one's real identity, and as something one must become through accomplishment, is undermined and rejected. One's real identity consists in fusion with mother, which one once had and would still have if the father had not stolen it away. This self would be without boundaries; boundaries would not only have been unnecessary to develop, but would get in the way.

What we can see here, obviously, is the root of the pristine self. Looking at the matter more broadly, we can see the dynamic underlying the anti-bullying movement. It is a maternal movement based on the image of the omnipotent mother, whose absolute love is not only possible, but also natural and normal. Creating boundaries in the face of an unloving world is not something one must do.

On the contrary, the unlovingness of the world is already an expression of its corruption. Dislike, or even indifference, is an act of offense; of bullying. This is why bullying is seen as ubiquitous. None of us lives in the world all by ourselves. We live among others. But if we take ourselves as the pristine self, the existence of others must be experienced as an attack, as bullying. So we experience bullying as omnipresent because others are omnipresent.

Now, in saying this, I do not wish to deny that there are acts of bullying and that there are bullies. There certainly are, and as such they are lamentable. What I am trying to explain is the way such acts are now seen as ubiquitous, even in the face of the fact that they are no more common than they ever were. I am trying to understand why they are seen as having a unity to them, as a malignant social phenomenon that is to be found everywhere and must be destroyed by contrary benevolent social phenomena.

This is an important difference. As I have said, there are, as there always have been, acts of bullying, and they are as lamentable as they have always been. Seeing them as omnipresent is quite something else. As I have argued, it is based on a normalization of the pristine self, driven by the dynamics of anti-Oedipal psychology. Looked at that way, the anti-bullying movement may be seen, itself, as an expression of anti-Oedipal psychology; and its benevolence, which is so easy to take for granted, cannot be assumed.

My purpose in what follows is to call that benevolence into question by showing what is at issue in anti-Oedipal psychology—the attack upon the father. I want to explore how the anti-bullying movement, seen in this way, can have adverse social consequences, and serious ones at that, even leading, perhaps, to an increase in bullying, not as an increase in individual incidence, but, ironically, as a universal form.

The Pristine Self and Social Interaction

If the anti-bullying movement simply noted that people are sometimes overly aggressive toward one another, and called for them to cut it out, no problem would arise. The problems come from the fact that it demands a pattern of social interaction based on the normality of the pristine self, experiencing the world from within primary narcissism. From within this framework, all acts that are not loving are seen as part of a pattern of oppression; all are of a piece, and all are, equivalently, bullying.

But this is a model that is inconsistent with civilized social interaction; it cannot be realized. It makes demands on us that cannot be satisfied and backs these demands with threats of powerful social sanctions, up to and including the power of the law. It thus institutionalizes organized coercion to which we must all be subject. Far from abolishing bullying, this is a setup for making it universal.

The anti-bullying movement undermines social structure. The maternal approach to the self normalizes the pristine self and primary narcissism. Within its embrace, we are all transcendentally important. The world is organized with love around each and every one of us. But each of us has what we see as the predominant place in this; others should revolve around us. The problem, of course, is that they make exactly the same demands on us. This would be a circle that has its center everywhere. One can see that this would be as contradictory for social order as it is for geometry.

Hobbes engaged with this matter in Leviathan (1651). There, he noted that there are three sources of discord among men: competition, distrust, and glory. The third is most relevant to us. He says

> Glory: Every man wants his associates to value him as highly as he values himself; and any sign that he is disregarded or undervalued naturally leads a man to try, as far as he dares, to raise his value in the eyes of others. For those who have disregarded him, he does this by violence; for others, by example. I say "as far as he dares"; but when there is no common power to keep them at peace, "as far as he dares" is far enough to make them destroy each other. That is why men don't get pleasure (and indeed do get much grief) from being in the company of other men without there being a power that can over-awe them all.

But of course if every subject is pristine, there cannot be a common power to "over-awe them all." The result must be that

> for as long as men live without a common power to keep them all in awe, they are in the condition known as "war"; and it is a war of every man against every man.

From which, he concluded:

> Therefore, whatever results from a time of war, when every man is enemy to every man, also results from a time when men live with no other security but what their own strength and ingenuity provides them with. In such conditions there is no place for hard work, because there is no assurance that it will yield results; and consequently no cultivation of the earth, no navigation or use of materials that can be imported by sea, no construction of large buildings, no machines for moving things that require much force, no knowledge of the face of the earth, no account of time, no practical

> skills, no literature or scholarship, no society; and—worst of all—continual fear and danger of violent death, and the life of man solitary, poor, nasty, brutish, and short.

This is a point that Hobbes made for politics, but it can also be made for consciousness, as Hegel (1964) did. When two consciousnesses come together, there is a fight to the death. I engage the world with myself as the locus of reference, and you do so as well. My affirmation of myself requires that the world be organized around me. As a result, your similar affirmation that it should be organized around you is experienced as threatening and intolerable. Hence, the duel to the death, in which each attempts to replace the other, in the mind of the other, with themselves. Each attempts, that is to say, to destroy the self-concept of the other. And it does not go too far to say that the methodology here is bullying, which we can see would be the universal form of social interaction.

Now, Hobbes's proposes an answer to this lamentable state of affairs. It is the Sovereign, the common power who will keep us all in awe. But does this put an end to universal bullying? I think not. Bullying is still ubiquitous, it is just that it is done by a hegemonic, unitary bully.

The Emergence of Civilization from the Primal Horde

So what can be done about this? How can civilized social order be possible? The psychoanalytically inclined will recognize that Freud (1913) dealt with exactly this question and had an answer. He offered the hypothesis, which works much better as phenomenology than as history, of a primordial horde under the domination of the primal father, who had exclusive access to everything good. We can see that he had the form of the Hobbesian Sovereign, the hegemonic bully, who kept them all in awe, and provided the basis for social order, tyrannical though it was.

But of course his sons didn't like his bullying any better than anyone else would, so they killed him. The result was, however, that they felt guilty. They resolved this by cooking the old man and eating him up; they internalized him, in other words. Freud's claim was that this internalization was the basis for social order of a new sort, which may call civilization, and in the course of this established a social order that was not based on bullying.

But what exactly were they internalizing, and how did it create the possibility of civilized social order?

The answers to these questions require some elaboration.

The Father of the Primal Horde

There is no need to go into great detail here on Freud's story of the primal horde. The primal father is a father, but a bad father. He is a tyrant who possesses everything in the group, most notably all the women and keeps control of all good things, offering no possibilities to anyone else. Freud tells us in *Group Psychology and the Analysis of the Ego* (1922a) that he is a monster:

> the father of the primal horde was free. His intellectual acts were strong and independent even in isolation, and his will needed no reinforcement from others. Consistency leads us to assume that his ego had few libidinal ties; he loved no one but himself, or other people only in so far as they served his needs. To objects his ego gave away no more than was barely necessary.

The sons, as we know, hated him for this and killed him. But they also loved him. So, Freud's story goes on to say, they felt remorse, cooked him, and ate him.

But of course, as Freud tells us in *Totem and Taboo* (1913), that was not the end of the matter:

> each was the other's rival among the women. Each one wanted to have them all to himself like the father, and in the fight of each against the other the new organization would have perished. For there was no longer any one stronger than all the rest who could have successfully assumed the rôle of the father.

Compare it with this from Hobbes

> for as long as men live without a common power to keep them all in awe, they are in the condition known as "war"; and it is a war of every man against every man.

The father, that is to say, through his strength, organized social activity. The principle of organization was his whim, his impulse; to use a term we do not much use these days, his id. When the sons killed him, there no longer was such a principle of organization because none of them could make his whim dominant. This is from *Moses and Monotheism* (Freud 1939):

> It is a reasonable surmise that after the killing of the father a time followed when the brothers quarrelled among themselves for the succession, which each of them wanted to obtain for himself alone. They came to see that these fights were as dangerous as they were futile. This hard-won understanding as well as the memory of the deed of liberation they had achieved together and the attachment that had grown up among them during the time of their exile led at last to a union among them, a sort of social contract

And, from *Totem and Taboo* again

> Though the brothers had joined forces in order to overcome the father, each was the other's rival among the women. Each one wanted to have them all to himself like the father, and in the fight of each against the other the new organization would have perished. For there was no longer any one stronger than all the rest who could have successfully assumed the rôle of the father.
>
> Thus there came into being the first form of a social organization accompanied by a renunciation of instinctual gratification; recognition of mutual obligations; institutions declared sacred, which could not be broken—in short the beginnings of morality and law.

The first act, I call it the *organic act*, of this social organization was the prohibition of incest:

> Thus there was nothing left for the brothers, if they wanted to live together, but to erect the incest prohibition—perhaps after many difficult experiences—through which they all equally renounced the women whom they desired, and on account of whom they had removed the father in the first place.(*ibid.*)

We must now stop and see what we have got here. The organizing principle in the primal horde was the father's whim. Now it is something quite different. It has become the collective, intentional action of an institution, in which each is recognized as being equally the father. It was thus based on an abstraction, a convention

In the horde, the principle of organization was the father, now it became the paternal function. Instead of being the father, the sons recognized each other as acting *in the name of the father*, to use Lacan's felicitous phrase; adopting the *role* of the father, the *function* of the father, in the task of organizing society.

What was created here was what I have called objective self-consciousness. The governance by the brothers was based, not on themselves, in some immediate sense, but *on an idea of themselves* that was created under the premise, and with the full mutual recognition, of being the same for each of them. It was the idea of themselves as members of the group.

It was only through the establishment of this identity for themselves that they were able to create and recognize their collective interest in denying the women to themselves and establishing the incest taboo.

Freud clearly believed that this creation of equality and mutual recognition therein was the organizing principle of primitive society.[5] And it was also clear that he located it as the most fundamental layer of social organization even unto this day; the Aristotelian *hypokaimenon*, so to speak.

One can see this most clearly by recognizing that the scope of the group in which one conceives one's membership is indefinitely elastic; at the most comprehensive, it refers to the designation "human being." It is, furthermore, subject to revision on the basis of experience, not least the experience of change brought about though transformations of ourselves through self-learning. And this experience of ourselves is not experience of ourselves in a vacuum, but in interaction with what is not ourselves; in a word, learning about ourselves means also learning about everything else as well.

One cannot overestimate the importance of this development. It is nothing short of the development of language. Through it, language is grounded in symbolism. To use the contemporary term, signifier and signified are established in mutual definition. Up until this point, words were just behavior; now they have come to *mean* something. The point is that they have come to mean *some*thing, and not *any*thing. If they meant *any*thing, they would mean *no*thing, simply being instances of themselves, as one finds in the word-salad of psychotics.

Thus, it is because they mean something that those things that are signified by a signifier can be contrasted with those that are not, and the process of learning about reality, and indeed creating reality, can begin.

What is specifically important for our purpose is that this organic act of mutual self-definition, the creation of objective self-consciousness, is at the same time the creation of law, of social order, and of organization. Through it, we become mutually predictable and accountable. It becomes possible to form rules of exchange and to coordinate our actions with one another.

So, to conclude, if Hobbes is correct that the state of war is the normal state, what keeps us out of it is the mutual internalization of the meaning of the father's role, the paternal function.

The problem that develops for our current concern is that the anti-Oedipal psychology inherent in the anti-bullying movement is an attack upon the paternal function. So, implicitly, the anti-bullying movement represents an attack against the foundation of social order.

To explore the meaning of this, and to generalize the matter beyond the dynamics of the primal horde, we need to go back again through the Oedipus complex. I want to add a view here that is derived from Chasseguet-Smirgel (1988).

The Father and Social Order

The story of the resolution of the Oedipus complex told above focuses on the boy. The place of the girl is rather different. In Freud's account, the girl's response to the threat of castration is that it has already happened. Lacking a penis, she cannot become like the father, but must become dependent upon him, until, ultimately, her male child will serve as a penis. This is a view, of course, that has been roundly rejected by women, who have objected to the image of women as passive and dependent on men.

Chasseguet-Smirgel's approach was not so much to deny Freud's account, but to psychoanalyze it. Her central insight is that the image of the passive, dependent female is the exact opposite of the omnipotent maternal imago that we all carry around with us, which we discussed above. The maternal imago is the root of our sense of being lovable. She thus controls how we feel about ourselves, which makes her, by far, the most powerful image in the psyche. It must have been that Freud's account had the unconscious purpose of denying this power.

We can understand why. The heart of all of our desire, whether we are male or female is the fantasy of returning to primary narcissism and fusing again with this powerful and wonderful figure. But such fusion also means the obliteration of the individual self. Our dependence on her is total, but she can abandon us at her whim, leaving us absolutely abject and bereft, undermining the very foundation of the meaning of our life. Freud repressed all this because it terrified him, as it terrifies all men. For men, the equation can be written that love equals death.

But that is not true for women. The little girl can live with this situation relatively easily. The mother's power over her is awesome, but she can counter it because, in her imagination, she shares it. She can see herself becoming a mother herself, and in that way gaining the power she needs to mitigate her mother's power over her.

But the boy cannot do that. What is he to do? He must, in his imagination, find a way to attain countervailing power over the mother, based on a dependency that she recognizes. He must do something she values enough to want to keep him around. But he must do this without the conscious recognition that this is what he is doing, which would maintain for him the terror that must always accompany his position.

I have argued (2003, 2010) that this is the meaning of male work. Work, as I am using the term here, refers to transactions defined within a framework of exchange. As such, it has certain characteristics that derive from the dynamics of this masculine position, and that cannot be accounted for in any other way. Most important is the necessity to act outside of the emotional realm, in the world of mutual indifference. This is made necessary by the fact that the emotional realm, dominated by the relationship with mother, is too dangerous. The positive side of this is that it makes possible the impersonality that Max Weber saw as the key to formal organization. Impersonality makes it possible to design and coordinate work activity to accomplish a purpose, and to adapt to circumstances, rather than having its direction monopolized by desire.

The impersonality that makes organization possible is made comprehensible by objective self-consciousness, and hence the paternal function. It is what makes it possible to develop rules that will apply to all of us, and in that way to be able to predict and coordinate with each other. As I have argued, the sons of the primal father learned to deal with each other on the basis of relative equality because each recognized that the others had internalized the paternal function, in the same way that they had. This mutual internalization has made possible the acceptance of joint responsibility for the organization of the group, which in turn has made possible the adoption of, and common agreement to be bound by, norms, and hence civilized social structure.

In all of this work, the object is to create something that the woman desires, which, as I have argued (2003), is simply to be herself. That is, her desire is to be what she is in her fantasy of the maternal imago: loving and omnipotent through her love. The meaning of the man's work, then, is to create a space within which she can simply be herself, hoping that within this space she will love him and they will fuse. In other words, his aim is to create a boundary between the sphere of the operation of her love, and the harsh and unloving world outside of it. In the classic case, we refer to this space as home, and the products of their fusion as their children.

Returning to our subject, it also makes possible, not so much the elimination of bullying among children, but outgrowing bullying by becoming an adult. It makes it possible to place in proportion the various slights and insults that all human beings encounter. This sense of proportion does not exist for the pristine self because, within its cosmic significance, all slights take on the identical cosmic significance.

Anti-Oedipal Psychology and the Destruction of the Paternal Function

We can now see what danger there is in anti-Oedipal psychology and the establishment of the pristine self. The primordial mother vouches for our importance and guarantees our safety. That is what she is created to do. However, she is not a real mother, but the fantasy of a mother that brings forward the time when mother was the world and loved us absolutely. Her meaning, therefore, is to make us safe as we carry primary narcissism forward and grow into what would otherwise be adulthood.

By committing ourselves to the normalization of this state, and committing ourselves to discredit or punish any impingement upon this pristine self, we, in effect, take over the function of this primordial mother. We enable infantilism.

Rejecting and destroying the father means the repudiation of the paternal function, which after all tells us that we are not center of the universe, which makes it possible to understand ourselves in universalistic terms. The internalization of the paternal function is what we mean by becoming an adult. Only within adulthood can we step outside of ourselves and recognize that narcissism is narcissism. In that way we can temper the tendencies that grow out of it, including, ironically, bullying.

For this reason, we must temper the wish to enable the normalization of the pristine self among our children. We must recognize the grandiosity, and, on many levels, lack of realism it involves. The alternative here is to arrogate to ourselves power beyond what we can wisely use, and put ourselves in the position of hegemonic control that, historically, only the worst of bullies have possessed.

Let me illustrate some of this reasoning through the case of Phoebe Prince.

Nightmare at South Hadley High

On 14 January 2010, Phoebe Prince, a Massachusetts high school student, committed suicide, ostensibly having been bullied to death. The case became an instant cause célèbre.

Prince first came to public attention through an article in the *Boston Globe* entitled The Untouchable Mean Girls by Kevin Cullen (2010). As Cullen recounts, her troubles grew out of the fact that she was a freshman who had a "brief fling" with a senior football player. Evidently, this was an intolerable violation of the norms of status for which the "Mean Girls" decided that she would have to be punished. The "Mean Girls," according to Cullen, took the nastiness that teenagers can display toward one another and raised it to a new level. They called her a slut and even an Irish slut. Finally, one of them, while driving with Phoebe on her way home, insulted her and threw an energy drink can toward her. When she arrived home after this, Phoebe killed herself. The Mean Girls denied responsibility for her suicide and mocked her in social media.

A local TV station came to interview some of the students and one girl said that it was common knowledge that bullies were "stalking the corridors" of South Hadley High School. Immediately after the TV crew left, according to Cullen, one of the Mean Girls threw the interviewee against a locker and punched her in the head.

Phoebe had been done in by an evil force, it thus appeared. Yet, evil as they were, these bullies appeared to be untouchable; they were unpunished and left free to continue their depredations. People were in denial. Rather than confronting the bullies who were roaming the halls, they blamed the victims, finding reasons why Phoebe would do this to herself.

For Cullen, this was a condition that could only have resulted from failure on the part of school administrators to do their job. Actually, school officials had launched three investigations of the matter, though none had yet come to fruition. They protested that more time was needed, but Cullen was not impressed; their continued presence was inexplicable. And he quoted a high school parent who wondered how many kids were not coming forward because they could see that the bullies had been left untouched.

The tide of opinion set in motion by Cullen's article helps to explain why, when District Attorney (DA) Elizabeth Scheidle filed felony charges against six of them, including a charge against five of them for "civil rights violation" for calling her an Irish slut, "involving bodily injury", that being her suicide, which could put them in prison for up to ten years,[6] her charges ran to great, even though not unanimous, applause.

A subsequent investigative report for *Slate* magazine by Emily Bazelon (2011) puts quite a different light on the matter. As it turns out, Prince, a recent immigrant from Ireland, had an unstable family and a history of cutting herself. She was a drug user, both of the illegal kind and of psychoactive medication for depression, a regimen that had recently seen an upgrade from Prozac to Seroquel (quetiapine), an antipsychotic. In fact, she had recently attempted suicide, before the advent of extreme bullying, by swallowing her bottle of Seroquel.

Interviewing kids and going over police interviews, Bazelon found that Prince was a bit more of an actor in this drama than had previously been recognized. For one thing, her "brief fling," as Cullen put it, was a good deal more offensive and egregious, in the eyes of her fellow students, than outside adults would recognize. It appears he, Austin, had a serious relationship with another girl, Flannery, who meant a great deal to him, and this relationship was helping him to turn his life around.

> "Austin was an angry kid for a long time," one of the adults at the school says. "But he had really come a long way. He was poised to get his diploma at the end of the summer. This thing with Phoebe, it appeared to throw him. Because he seemed really committed to Flannery. She was pretty well grounded and she had good connections in school with other adults. I think she was good for Austin."

In fact, generally, far from a solitary girl who was new to the school and set upon by an established bunch of mean, jealous kids for one relationship, Prince was seen as a threat to *everyone's* relationships. She was drawing guys to her on a wholesale level and was widely seen as the predator. Despite her lowly status, it was she, and not the bullies, who was seen as having the power. Indeed, the Mean Girls appear to have been acting, not on their own behalf, but in defense of the whole group.

The day of her suicide, all agree, was the period of the worst bullying she received. She went to the library during lunch and sat next to a friend and a senior boy who was helping her with math. Sean, Kayla, and Ashley were sitting at a nearby table and one of them wrote "Irish bitch is a cunt" next to her name in the signup sheet. Ashley yelled some insults at her, calling her a whore and a stupid slut and telling her to close her legs. She encountered this group again, at the end of the day, on her way to the parking lot. Evidently, Sean said, "Here she comes," Ashley called her a whore, and the others laughed. As she walked home, Ashley drove by in a friend's car, yelled "whore" out the window, and threw an empty drink can at her.

A few hours later, she hanged herself, but it is worth asking whether, if she had not hanged herself, that episode would have seemed extraordinary. The fact is that most of the bullying was stuff like this:

> One night in early January, Flannery made an apparent reference to Phoebe on her Facebook page. In an exchange with another girl who brought up an event they'd both attended, Flannery replied, "Hahaha best night of my life :) ya we kick it with the true irish not the gross slutter poser ones :)." A third girl asked if she counted as cute and Irish, and a fourth one chimed in "like meeee :)." Flannery answered, "Yes I love you … I think you no who im talking about:)." A couple of girls replied with a chorus of "hahas."

Having looked at the whole picture, what strikes me about this is the banality of it all. Even the worst of the bullying seems, to me, to be well within the normal range of cruelties that teenagers inflict upon one another. This is a judgment with which the teenagers themselves seemed to agree. For them, calling a girl out as a slut was not exactly condoned, but it wasn't far from it. Kids said nasty things to each other all the time. This was universally known and, for that reason, not taken all that seriously.

> One 18-year-old said she heard Kayla privately call Phoebe a "whore who wanted attention." "I didn't take what Kayla said that seriously because girls in my school get in 'bitch fights' all the time," she told the police.

Bazelon notes the contrasts between the students' reality, based on her interviews and those of the police, and the official picture, as presented in the public statement of DA Elizabeth Scheibel justifying the filing of felony charges against the six students. Scheibel characterized the bullying as a "nearly three-month campaign" of "relentless" and "torturous" bullying. But Bazelon found no evidence of an organized campaign, nor of anything that lasted anywhere near that long. Scheibel said of the teens:

"Their conduct far exceeded the limits of normal teenage relationship-related quarrels." Bazelon observes that this point was crucial to Scheibel's decision to prosecute, but she found no agreement among the teenagers she talked to that what happened to Prince was particularly unusual. To them, this was just "ordinary girl drama," and, indeed, though nobody wanted to blame the girl who died, drama to which Prince made her own contribution.

"Each person had his own conflict with Phoebe—that's what no one outside our school seems to understand," says Christine, the friend of Sean's and Austin's. "The girls found out she'd been with the boys, and true to high-school girls, they got mad at the girl instead of the boyfriend."

Let me be clear what I am saying here. I am not saying that Prince's death was not tragic, nor that the bullying that preceded it was not condemnable. Prince was certainly very unhappy and the bullying certainly contributed to that. The question I am raising is whether these specific behaviors justified the lurid presentation of school life as dominated by untamed bands of bullies, roving the halls, and committing unprovoked depredations at their whim, or were within the spectrum of ordinary disorganized spontaneous behavior characteristic of students in that age range. Bazelon's evidence inclines us toward the latter possibility.

The question that brings up is where the idea of bullying as a unitary, malignant force, from which Prince could not escape, came from. I think we get a leg up on this by considering that the worst case of bullying, described above, came from only three of the students charged, while the felony charges, five of which were identical, were leveled against six students, and included behavior that was not extraordinarily cruel by any measure. Evidently, then, in the mind of the DA, the mildest of the acts of bullying were seen in the same way as the most egregious. The only way one can see such mild behavior as seriously offensive is by looking at them in the context of a self that is infinitely susceptible to abuse because it is categorically vulnerable to any expression of offense and totally incapable of defending itself, and that has a narcissistic premise to it that sees a unity in these expressions of offense that is not necessarily there.

That is what I call the pristine self, and it is, I submit, the image of the self in the mind of the DA, who, ironically, was here acting as hegemonic bully.

So if what we are seeing in the Prince case is not an expression of bullying as an organized malignant social force, what is it?

I suggest that it is no more or less than the social sanctioning through which norms are enforced. Moreover, the norm that was being enforced was an important one, and one that is hard to imagine being enforced in any other way.

That norm is the expression of a belief that sexual activity should be organized in a certain way. Beginning with the incest taboo, the psychoanalytic model, and not only the psychoanalytic model, says that society organizes itself by regulating who can have sex with whom. Such regulation is so critical because sex is not only about sex. Rather, the desire for sex being what it is, its regulation provides the leverage for determining family structure and kinship, which in turn determines the nature and meaning of work, and everything else that takes place within those contexts.

The normative structure of society is a product of the paternal function, but norms operate through feeling, not through thought. Society obviously cannot be dependent on all of its member being able to think such matters through. Rather, it transmits them, and must transmit them, through feelings of what is right and what is wrong.

And yet, it is clear, such transmission cannot help but involve pain. It ultimately has to be taught by subjecting individuals to sanctions, positive and negative, moral approval and disapproval, for upholding and violating the norms. But the burden of determination must fall on the negative of these. The positive is largely a matter of simple acceptance, which by definition does not stand out from the background.

These expressions of moral disapproval gain their strength, not so much as abstract judgments, but from individuals feeling that the organization of their own lives, including their security in the preservation of whatever good they have attained, including their erotic connections, is threatened by violation of these norms, especially when this impinges on their own case. This is going to be nasty, emotional stuff.

So how does a high school girl respond when a new girl comes to town from Ireland and starts sleeping with her boyfriend? Odds are she calls her an Irish slut. And when the new girl starts sleeping with a whole raft of such boyfriends, you find exactly the sort of thing that happened at South Hadley High School.

And so we have explained the case of Phoebe Prince, and have done so without once referring to bullying. But if that is so, then how did it happen that the concept of bullying was invoked here, and invoked in such a way as to establish a paradigm?

The answer I propose is, of course, that when we invoke the concept of omnipresent bullying, we are employing the idea of the pristine self, which is not our customary way of seeing ourselves, and not a very good one, given that we can explain even its paradigm cases without the use of it.

But if we look at the matter that way, we may recognize something very disturbing, which is that there is a conflict between the idea of the pristine self and the social processes though which norms are enforced, even the norms that are the most important. The concept of the pristine self, that is to say, makes social order impossible.

But reflection tells us that this was implicit right at the beginning. The pristine self is inherently narcissistic. The maternal other that guarantees the safety of this self is, in fact, not an other at all, but an infantile image of what an other ought to be, a complement to the infant's narcissism. There is, in this world, no possibility of real others. On the contrary, their very existence is an intrusion that shows up as bullying.

In short, it is easy to see that there cannot be social order on this premise. Either there is no social, in the sense that social involves the existence of others, or there is, as we saw before, no order. Such are the wages of the expulsion of the father.

Conclusion: The Case of Organizations

In concluding, I would like to draw some direct implications concerning the anti-bullying movement in organizations. Organizations are based on the paternal function, as it is manifest in rules that apply to everyone in a given status, irrespective of who they are. But this stands counter to the pristine self, to whom nothing can be higher than who they are. This will be so with regard to formal, but also informal rules, in the form of norms, which as we have seen fared badly at the hands of the anti-bullying movement.

The implication of this is that the anti-bullying movement, invoking the concept of the pristine self, poses a threat to organizations in general. As it turns out, there is an illustration of this at South Hadley High School.

In the wake of Prince's suicide, the school took a tremendous amount of heat. For example, Bazelon pointed to the case of Michael Cahillane, a protégé of DA Scheibel, who had been running to succeed her when she left office, and whose position was that the DA would not have to bring cases like this if the schools had been doing their jobs.

Bazelon thinks there is some merit in this. There were, it turns out, signals of Prince's suffering, and Bazelon takes seriously the charge that the school was not sufficiently aggressive in caring for her. Others say that school officials should have known more about the bullying that was underway and should have dealt with it.

But if the case simply involved teenagers being teenagers, which only looked problematic in retrospect, after the suicide, what exactly would they have had to be aware of?

If the involvement of the pristine self is the issue here, then the analysis of what signals were missed in the Prince case misses an important point. Anything can count as an assault on the pristine self, and if we are looking to outlaw anything that could set off anyone, that will come to include the fact that an organization is an organization.

Keep in mind that Prince was taking serious anti-depressant medication, and that this is one of the signals that was supposed to have alerted the school administration. But how would it have been with her if she had not been? Presumably, she would have been more depressed, but there would have been fewer signals. This raises the question what would an organization need to do in order to ensure that every member of the organization, even the most vulnerable, is not hurt? How much of its attention would need to be given over to identifying vulnerability?

One does not want to pretend to have knowledge where one has only conjectures, but it looks to me as if Prince belonged in a mental hospital. That would have been the level of attention that would have been appropriate to her condition. But can a high school function like a mental hospital? Can any organization? Should every organization have to become a mental hospital? What about the work that other kinds of organizations, dedicated to other purposes, perform in the normal course of their operations? And, finally, who will take care of those who are taking care? Why would they be less vulnerable than those in their charge?

The problem is that the pristine self is an absolute. Having no boundaries, the existence of a world outside itself is already an assault. Recognizing nothing outside itself, it cannot step outside itself and look at itself. For this reason, the pristine self does not have any way of assessing proportion; any violation can feel like an absolute. Yet if we are going to insure that nobody feels injury, we must assume that everyone is infinitely vulnerable.

If we raise up the pristine self as normal, learning how to cope becomes anomalous. We all become helpless children needing our mothers. But there are no such mothers and there never were.

Notes

1. I am grateful to Larry Hirschhorn for bringing this to my attention.
2. When I use the term pristine self, I am not referring not so much to a person, as to an *idea* of a person. A person operating with such openness would be without boundaries and quasi psychotic; the designation *borderline* makes especially good sense here (NIMH 2014). But the NIMH suggests an incidence of BPD in the USA of only 1.6 % in any given year. By itself, I don't believe that would account for the cultural shift I have in mind. And at any rate, I have never found it particularly useful to account for social phenomena through the diagnosis of individual pathology.
   For that purpose, I think it is much more useful to think of the pristine self as an idea of a person, a self-concept. The point here is that it is available for identification. The degree of identification can vary. At one extreme, we would find the classic borderline type. At another extreme, we could have what I think of as the pristine self by proxy, in which an identification with someone else arouses responses vicariously.
3. This is of course the little boy version. The little girl version will be addressed later.
4. See my *Revolt of the Primitive* (2003) for an extended treatment of this.
5. Interestingly, Freud's (1913) idea of equality in primitive organizations seemed to include women, though in a different way, through the institution of matriarchy, which he borrows from Bachoven. The result:

   > The most primitive organization we know, which to-day is still in force with certain tribes, is associations of men consisting of members with equal rights, subject to the restrictions of the totemic system, and founded on matriarchy, or descent through the mother.

6. In the end, all the students pleaded guilty to minor charges and received probation. In all but one case, the charges were to be expunged on satisfactory completion of probation.

References

Bazelon, E. 2011. What Really Happened to Phoebe Prince? *Slate Magazine*, July 20. http://www.slate.com/articles/life/bulle/features/2011/what_really_happened_to_phoebe_prince/the_untold_story_of_her_suicide_and_the_role_of_the_kids_who_have_been_criminally_charged_for_it.

Chasseguet-Smirgel, J. 1988. *Sexuality and Mind: The Role of the Father and the Mother in the Psyche*. London: Karnac.

Clark, Maggie. 2013. 49 States Now Have Anti-Bullying Laws. How's that Working Out? Governing the States and Localities. http://www.governing.com/news/headlines/49-States-Now-Have-Anti-Bullying-Laws-Hows-that-Working-Out.html.

Cullen, K. 2010. The Untouchable Mean Girls. *Boston Globe*, January 24. http://www.boston.com/news/local/massachusetts/articles/2010/01/24/the_untouchable_mean_girls/.

Finkelhor, David. 2013. Trends in Bullying and Peer Victimization. Crimes Against Children Research Center, University of New Hampshire, January. http://www.unh.edu/ccrc/pdf/CV280_Bullying%20&%20Peer%20Victimization%20Bulletin_1-23-13_with%20toby%20edits.pdf.

Freud, S. 1913. *Totem and Taboo*. London: Hogarth Press.

Freud, Sigmund. 1922a. *Group Psychology and the Analysis of the Ego*. London: Hogarth.

———. 1939. *Moses and Monotheism*. London: Hogarth.

Hegel, G.W.F. 1964. *The Phenomenology of Mind*. New York: Humanities Press.

Hobbes, Thomas. 1651. *Leviathan*. Amazon Kindle edition.

National Institute of Mental Health. 2014. Borderline Personality Disorder. http://www.nimh.nih.gov/health/topics/borderline-personality-disorder/index.shtml. Accessed 12 July 2014.

Schwartz, Howard S. 2003. *Revolt of the Primitive: An Inquiry Into the Roots of Political Correctness*. Piscataway, NJ: Transaction Publishers.

——— 2010. *Society Against Itself: Political Correctness and Organizational Decay*. London: Karnac.

Schwartz, John. 2010. Bullying, Suicide, Punishment. *New York Times*, October 2. http://www.nytimes.com/2010/10/03/weekinreview/03schwartz.html?_r=0.

CHAPTER 3

Putnam's Paradox: Diversity, Destruction of Community, and Anti-Oedipal Psychology

Analyzing the data from a large nationwide survey of the effects of diversity on social capital, the eminent political scientist Robert Putnam (2007) found some results that surprised and disturbed him.

The survey, with over 30,000 subjects in 41 communities, and with the level of specificity analyzable down to the census-tract neighborhood, defined social capital as "social networks and the associated norms of reciprocity and trustworthiness." Diversity was defined as it was in the concurrent US census in terms of these ethnic and racial categories: Hispanic, non-Hispanic white, non-Hispanic black, and Asian.

The idea behind the study was to determine whether attitudes of trust and social solidarity among in-groups would be inversely correlated with those toward out-groups. This had been assumed in the literature but never tested.

Putnam put this question in terms of two alternative hypotheses, in accordance with the main theories within the domain. One theory, called conflict theory, maintained that the presence of others would lead to hostility against them and lack of trust. In this theory, in-group solidarity would be enhanced by diversity, since it would lead to increased in-group cohesiveness, in the form of "bonding" social capital. The other theory, called the contact theory, assumes that contact with other groups would increase connections with them, enhancing trust and generating

H.S. Schwartz, *Political Correctness and the Destruction of Social Order*, DOI 10.1007/978-3-319-39805-1_3

"bridging" social capital, and that this would decrease the necessity to form in-group solidarity as a defensive formation.

Most previous research had generally confirmed conflict theory, suggesting that diversity would be correlated with lack of trust and solidarity with out-groups, and leading to the expectation that there would be an increase in the level of trust and solidarity among in-groups.

The first part of this expectation was fulfilled; as shown in Fig. 3.1, diversity negatively affected attitudes toward out-groups.

Putnam said of this:

> The more ethnically diverse the people we live around, the less we trust them. This pattern may be distressing normatively, but it seems to be consistent with conflict theory

However, the second was not. As shown in Fig. 3.2, diversity did not accentuate individuals' propensity to trust members of their own group; it decreased it. And this was the cause of Putnam's distress.

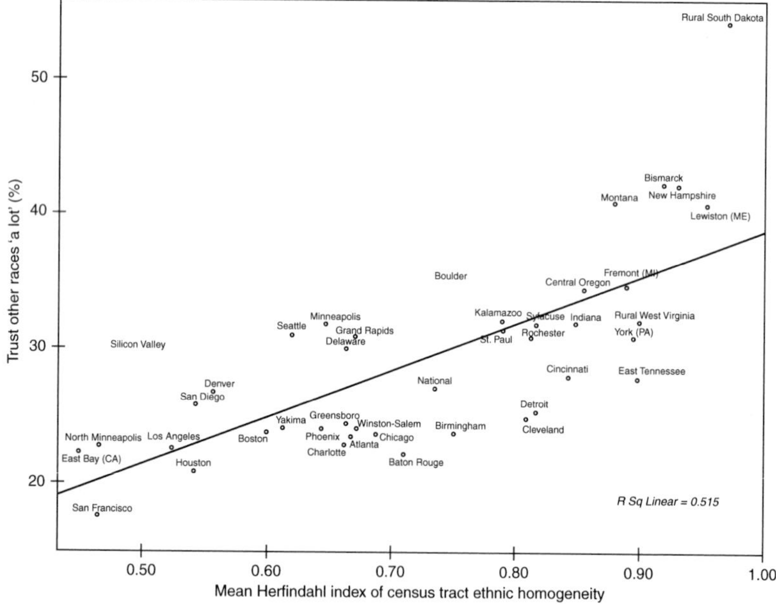

Fig. 3.1 Racial homogeneity and inter-racial trust

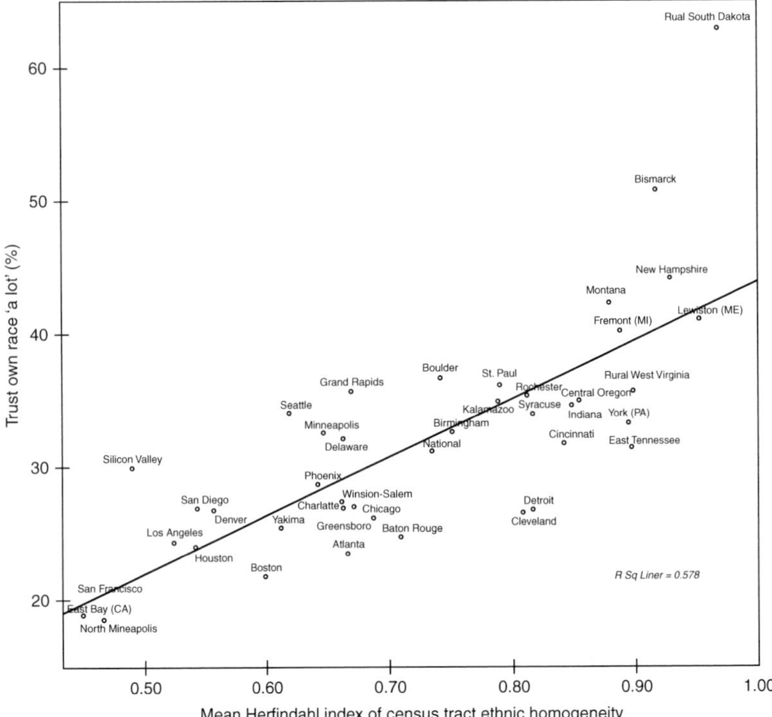

Fig. 3.2 Racial homogeneity and intra-racial trust

Now, when Putnam speaks of trust, he is not referring only to whether respondents say they trust specific others. What was at issue here was virtually the entire range of social engagement.

Persons living in areas of greater diversity had, among other things, lower trust in local government and leaders, lower expectations that others will cooperate to solve common problems, less altruism, and fewer friends. Virtually the only social activity enhanced by diversity was the tendency to participate in social protest.

Here is a list of correlates of diversity:

- Decreased confidence in local government, local leaders, and the local news media.

- Decreased political efficacy—that is, confidence in their own influence.
- Decreased frequency of registering to vote.
- Increased interest and knowledge about politics and more participation in protest marches and social reform groups.
- Diminished expectation that others will cooperate to solve dilemmas of collective action (e.g. voluntary conservation to ease a water or energy shortage).
- Diminished likelihood of working on a community project.
- Diminished likelihood of giving to charity or volunteering.
- Lower number of close friends and confidants.
- Lower level of happiness and lower perceived quality of life.
- More time spent watching television and more agreement that "television is my most important form of entertainment."

Now, there were significant limits to this compendium. In addition to the tendency toward political protest, listed above, Putnam also found that "organizational activity of various sorts, including religious activity" was uncorrelated with diversity. We will return to this, but for now we may turn to the conclusion that Putnam drew:

> Diversity seems to trigger not in-group/out-group division, but anomie or social isolation. In colloquial language, people living in ethnically diverse settings appear to 'hunker down'—that is, to pull in like a turtle. ... Diversity does not produce "bad race relations" or ethnically-defined group hostility, our findings suggest. Rather, inhabitants of diverse communities tend to withdraw from collective life, to distrust their neighbours, regardless of the colour of their skin, to withdraw even from close friends, to expect the worst from their community and its leaders, to volunteer less, give less to charity and work on community projects less often, to register to vote less, to agitate for social reform more, but have less faith that they can actually make a difference, and to huddle unhappily in front of the television. Note that this pattern encompasses attitudes and behavior, bridging and bonding social capital, public and private connections. Diversity, at least in the short run, seems to bring out the turtle in all of us. (149–150)

Now, for a man of Putnam's liberal political leanings, these findings were anathema. He suppressed his results for five years and, at a Harvard seminar before a select group, seemed to seriously consider the possibility of not publishing them at all. According to a participant:

> After finishing his presentation of the data, Putnam began a class discussion. He asked us whether we thought that all relevant scientific findings, no matter how disagreeable, deserve a public airing. Perhaps he was just trying to get us to think about difficult issues, but Putnam seemed genuinely conflicted himself. His concerns were rooted, understandably, in his personal politics. A man of the Left, he told us that he was deeply worried about being seen as advocating some form of "ethnic cleansing," or being associated with the far Right in general. (Richwine 2009)

When he did publish, he chose to publish only a brief summary of his findings, in an obscure journal, and without making his data available to other researchers. In the publication, he tried to hedge by starting and ending with arguments that diversity is inevitable and can have a positive impact, for example, by enhancing creativity; and that over the long term, the problems with diversity would take care of themselves through the formation of a new sense of "we."

But these were of no avail. An article in the *Financial Times* (Lloyd 2006) brought him out and enunciated the conclusion that Putnam was trying to keep quiet. The headline: "Study paints bleak picture of diversity."

The article's negative interpretation, which was taken up in numerous other outlets, left Putnam feeling quite abused. In an interview with the *Harvard Crimson* (Goldsmith 2006) he said it was "almost criminal" that the *FT* article did not emphasize his optimistic "conclusion." But his hesitation to publish suggests that he knew this would happen. His optimism, after all, was essentially an expression of piety and a testimonial of his faith. The significance of his article was in the empirical findings, about which Putnam was at a loss to account.[1]

Perhaps with a bit of psychoanalysis, we can help him out.

In what follows, I am going to offer an explanation of Putnam's findings based on psychoanalytic theory. The gap between the quantitative form of data Putnam offers, if not its content, and the abstract theorizing, invoking psychological processes of which there can be only inferential understanding, is very great. The connections I draw here are highly speculative, tentative, and exploratory. Further reflection, and perhaps further empirical analysis, may permit the strengthening of these connections; or it may dissipate them entirely.

For the time being, our purpose will be only to see how far an idea goes. Think of it as a game we are playing.

We will begin this game by going back over his article and his response to the response to it.

Reflecting on Putnam and His Findings

We note first that Putnam's objection to the *FT* gloss was that it was, in his view, misinterpreting his attitude, his feelings, rather than his empirical findings as such. Similarly, in the Harvard seminar he said he was "deeply worried about being seen as advocating some form of 'ethnic cleansing,' or being associated with the far Right in general."

He did not trust that his community would understand him as he needed to be understood. Whatever protestations he might make, he would be seen having a certain attitude, a certain set of feelings, and was afraid of being ostracized on the basis of that judgment about him. He was, in a word, afraid of being condemned for being politically incorrect.

We follow this by noting that his response to this potential condemnation of his politically incorrect feelings was to cut himself loose from the communication networks and social formations that structured his life as an academic. He had, in a word, "hunkered down."

Second, we recall that Putnam found that there was one form of social connection that was the opposite of the tendency to withdraw in the face of diversity. He said that increased diversity led to "more interest and knowledge about politics and more participation in protest marches and social reform groups."

I will suggest that Putnam has things upside down. My claim is that it is the political correlate of diversity, the politics of political correctness, and more precisely the psychological dynamics that underlie such politics that have been responsible for the breakdown of social connection rather than diversity itself.

The theoretical basis for this claim will be the theory of anti-Oedipal psychology which argues that the dynamic underlying political correctness is an attack upon the father, and specifically the paternal function.

In anti-Oedipal psychology, as we have seen, social order, which is brought about through the paternal function, is rejected in the name of a primitive mother who seeks to expel the father and his works in favor of her own omnipotence. It is not a far stretch to extend this to Putnam's findings on the breakdown of social capital and trust.

The gravamen of this argument is that it is the paternal function that makes it possible for people to engage with each other through a common framework of understanding, indeed a common language. This would be necessary for social trust and collective action.

Where this common framework of understanding is built into the structure of association, as it is in organizations, and especially where these organizations are firmly based in transcendent religious ideology, the corrosive effects of anti-Oedipal psychology are relatively, although perhaps temporarily, minimized, which is what Putnam found.

Oedipal Psychology and the Paternal Function

As we saw in Chap. 2, the child's early life is defined by its closeness and openness to mother; its fusion with her. The mother is the world to the child. She is experienced as pure, omnipotent goodness. Mother's love for the child is therefore experienced as being undifferentiated from the child itself, leaving the child as the center of a loving world. Its experience of its relationship with the world is that it can do what it wants and be loved for it.

The father makes his appearance as an intrusion into this idyll. He has a relationship with her that does not revolve around the child and therefore stands as a barrier between the child and mother. He thus puts an end to the child's primary narcissism. The father's *no* separates the child from this mother and what Lacan calls the *jouissance* of their connection.

And it's a good thing he does. The child's primary narcissism is a fantasy, which the father's intrusion into this configuration dispels; he represents the advent of reality.

But socialization cannot just be the outcome of prohibition. Otherwise, there could be no reason to do anything. There must be a ground for desire. This requirement is fulfilled by the ego ideal, a fantasy of return to primary narcissism, in the form of fusion with mother as, in the child's mind, the father has.

As I have said, within this configuration, the father gains his place with mother by creating conditions that allow mother to safely be her loving self. He can create a boundary between mother and the harsh, external reality that can punish her for her expression of love.

Now, the father does not create these conditions from within the sphere of mother's love, but outside of it, in the harsh objective reality that he is trying to create a boundary against.

His task, then, is to embrace the reality that it is his lot to represent; to learn about it and about how to accomplish something within it. What he learns will not be unique to him; he left his feeling of uniqueness behind him when he lost his primary narcissism in his own time. Others, therefore, will be able to find it to be as applicable as he does. We call this objective knowledge, in the sense that it is knowledge of the world as objects whose characteristics are not dependent on our subjective views of them.

The capacity of others to share this objective knowledge provides the basis for us to accomplish things jointly. Each knowing what the others know, we can predict and coordinate our behavior, establishing common purposes that help us all to further our individual purposes. When these patterns of coordination become regularized and formalized, we call them organizations. But this regularization takes place informally as well, constituting what Putnam calls social capital. For reasons he related to diversity, it has come under threat.

The substance of this mutual accretion is language, in a broad sense, or the symbolic, in Lacan's term. The symbolic consists here in the common understandings, rules, obligations, and so on that a member of the society possesses or that he, in principle, can possess, and which serve as the architecture of his view of life and provide for his place within it.

I have referred to the core of this as "objective self-consciousness," which is a way of seeing oneself within the symbolic; not so much as one really is, but as an object, as someone else would see you who was not emotionally connected with you.

It is the symbolic; language, objective self-consciousness, the legacy of the father, and the instantiation of the paternal function that has made social capital possible. In everything less primitive than the fantasy connection of mother and child, everything from marriage to the structure of whole societies, ways of engaging with each other based on common understandings, obligations, and so on provide the structure out of which connections are made.

My claim is that the breakdown in social capital that Putnam found is a result of the weakening of the symbolic, a breakdown of common understanding. As the father was the creator of the symbolic, so its breakdown has been the product of the assault upon the father that has been the dominant cultural movement of our time. To make this case, I will need to turn to the analysis of political correctness and the anti-Oedipal psychology that has brought this about.

Anti-Oedipal Psychology and the Destruction of the Paternal Function

Objective self-consciousness is a developmental achievement. In contrast to it is a more primitive conception of ourselves in what Lacan called the imaginary, which is inherently subjective and fictional, as Lacan understood an image in a mirror to be.

The imaginary, which is the locus of our feelings and emotions, is structurally narcissistic, since our feelings and emotions are, after all, *our* feelings and emotions. They are not symbols. Through them, we do not refer to anything; they simply are what they are. Language, if such it may be called, is entirely self-referential.

The imaginary is presided over by the primitive mother, whose love validates us in our individuality. She provides support for our spontaneous impulse, implicitly offering the guarantee that we can safely do what we want because the world is organized around us with love.[2]

Political correctness is a bid for hegemony in the name of this primitive mother, expelling the father and undermining the paternal function. As such, it is a bid for the destruction of the symbolic.

The problem is that the loss of the paternal function and the symbolic deprives us of the structure that the symbolic provides. Society is recast on the basis of Putnam's "hunkered down" individuals, who define themselves in terms of the pristine self, and are therefore deeply unconnected to each other.

This disorganization takes place internally as well as externally. For Lacan, the loss of the symbolic, the unconstrained playing out of the imaginary, is psychosis.

When I use the term psychosis, I am not using it loosely, although the locus of my analysis is the societal level, not the individual. My point here is that the mind and reality are coming undone, and the result must be the disordering of the psyche. I will illustrate this through the concept of the transgendered person.

Consider the case of Bruce Jenner, who now declares that he wants to be called Catelyn. I personally would be perfectly happy to call him Catelyn, if I ever met him, or anything else that he would like. But the problem is not what he wants to be called, but how he wants people to *think* of him. He wants people to think of him as a woman and, what's most important, he wants people to think that he has *always been* a woman. And people go along with it. That way madness lies.

He is a woman in a man's body, he says. But what does it mean to be a woman in a man's body? If it is not a person's body that determines their sex, what can it be? What can it mean to say that a body is a woman's body if the person with that body can be a man? In what sense is it a woman's body? It seems that the words "man" and "woman" have lost their meaning. To say that someone is a man in a woman's body is to say nothing at all, nor is it saying anything to say that someone is a man or a woman.

What else could define one's sex? Could it be one's feelings? But feelings can change from day to day, or minute to minute. If your sex is determined by your feelings, it must be subject to change every minute. But that is to say that you have no sex. Worse, it could mean that the sex you have in the minute is the sex you have had all along. One must be reminded here of Orwell: Eastasia has always been at war with Oceania. What other model can we use for asserting that Bruce Jenner has always been a woman?

In the tradition of Saussure, Lacan maintained that language is mostly about other language. We live within a chain of signifiers. The term "man," for example, is partly constituted in contrast with the term "woman." But language cannot just be about other language. It must touch the ground someplace if it is going to be useful in relating to the world at all. So there must be and there are points where it *does* touch the world. Lacan calls these *points de caption*, anchoring points, where "signified and signifier are knotted together." (1993, p. 268). The absence of these points defines psychosis.

Now, my contention is that terms like man and woman are anchoring points of this sort. Am I a boy or a girl, the child wants to know, and the answer to this helps him to build a sense of himself in relation to the world, and an idea of what he is supposed to do in it. Take that away and the mind, and life itself, lose their moorings, coming to float freely wherever the currents of language, and the cultural institutions that direct and channel those currents, quite without accountability, and these days under the dominion of political correctness, take them. What disappears here is our mutual capacity to predict and coordinate with each other, which is the heart of organized social life at every level.

Political Correctness and the Pristine Self

I have argued elsewhere that political correctness is an attack against the father, and specifically the paternal function—the authority taken in the name of the father to create, define, transmit, and renew objective self-consciousness—that is the target of political correctness.

Putting the matter briefly, this attack is undertaken in the name of the primordial mother who is omnipotent, who loves us entirely, and who would bring back the blissful state of primary narcissism, in which we were the center of a loving world, were it not for the fact the father has stolen her love from us. Getting rid of him will realize the ego ideal. We will be free of the demands and expectations placed upon us by our mutual acceptance of objective self-consciousness. We will not be subordinate to any roles, rules, or obligations, but will be able to do what we want, act on our whim, in perfect safety, to the accompaniment of mother's love.

What the father claims as objective self-consciousness is only the expression of his own subjectivity. The accomplishments the father has wrought through the construction and renewal of objective self-consciousness, and through his transformation of the world created and defined in this way, are redefined as without value; they are just ways in which he justified his theft and through which he justified his claim to her love.

The father stole mother's love from all of us children, but most massively from those who have been specifically deprived of her love through what are seen as the modalities of oppression. It is therefore righteous to hate him for his theft and to love those who have been oppressed, in compensation.

That is the basic dynamic of political correctness. I call the psychology that underlies it anti-Oedipal, in that it is the reverse of the Oedipal process in which the children identify with the father and internalize the social and intellectual orders that are the products of the paternal function. Within Oedipal psychology, the route to the ego ideal is through becoming like the father. In anti-Oedipal psychology, the route to the ego ideal is through destroying the father and the paternal function.

As I have said, the rejection of objective self-consciousness under the protection of the primordial mother corresponds to a concept of the self that is the reverse of objective self-consciousness, which I call the pristine self, a self that is untouched by anything but love.

In general, for a person holding the pristine idea of himself, anything but love would be experienced as a violation of an absolute entitlement.

Since this way of seeing oneself is profoundly narcissistic, such violations would be felt to be personal attacks. Even the indifferent aspects of reality, such as, perhaps most importantly, the fact that most other people, most of the time, do not give a damn about us as individuals, would be experienced as intolerable. Given one's assumption of one's own goodness, the natural response to these feelings of violation would be either righteous rage, or, alternatively, the deflation of the sense of one's goodness.

The loss of objective self-consciousness, the loss of a mutual conception that people act according to shared principles of behavior, makes the mutual predictability and coordination that this brought about impossible.

But for our purposes the crucial loss here is psychology; the sense, however implicit and underdeveloped, that people are what they are and do what they do because they are people, and that being a person means acting in accordance with objective determinants that affect everybody.

My sense of who I am, my ego, is the central reference point of my life. Objective self-consciousness involves, or at least permits, the recognition that this is true of everyone. The alternative that shows up in the pristine self is that my centrality in my own life is not matched by other people's centrality in theirs, but is replicated directly. They are not the centers of their own lives, but I am. People acting for their own reasons, people taking themselves as their central reference instead of taking me as their central reference, becomes incomprehensible, and signs of it are experienced as violations of the proper order of things.

Such a person would find the existence of other minds intolerable. They would experience the world as a locus of ubiquitous threat, organized against them, leading to an approach to the world that we can only call paranoid.

I do not use this word lightly. Freud's analysis of paranoia comes strikingly close to what we have here. He says (1922b):

> We are reminded that sufferers from persecutory paranoia … cannot regard anything in other people as indifferent, and they, too, take up minute indications with which these other, unknown, people present them, and use them in their delusions of reference. The meaning of their delusion of reference is that they expect from all strangers something like love. … and, considering, too, the fundamental kinship of the concepts of "stranger" and "enemy,"

> the paranoic is not so far wrong in regarding this indifference as hate, in contrast to his claim for love.

But Freud's analysis can be taken farther, bringing us back to Putnam. He says with regard to the Schreber case (1911), that in the normal course of heterosexual development, homosexual libido is detached from the individual's narcissistic fixation on himself and given new directions.

> homosexual tendencies are … deflected from their sexual aim and applied to fresh uses. They now combine[s] with portions of the ego-instincts and, as "attached" components, help to constitute the social instincts, thus contributing an erotic factor to friendship and comradeship, to esprit de corps and to the love of mankind in general. How large a contribution is in fact derived from erotic sources (with the sexual aim inhibited) could scarcely be guessed from the normal social relations of mankind.

But, in the case of paranoia, homosexual libido, along with all other libido, is withdrawn from the world and focused, again, on the self. As Freud puts it:

> According to our analytic view the megalomania is the direct result of a magnification of the ego due to the drawing in of the libidinal object-cathexes—a secondary narcissism which is a return of the original early infantile one. (1917)

Applying all this to Putnam's findings, we would not be surprised to find that these people would not get along too well and would tend not to form voluntary associations. This is why organizations like religious organizations, inheriting a structure, and perhaps a foundational sacred ideology, from previous times, and not as subject to spontaneous reformulation as newly formed organizations are, would be relatively exempt from the deterioration Putnam found.

But we can understand that the more important exception would be political associations, where they could identify with each other in their mutual experience of being threatened and identify a unified cause that they could righteously fight against.

I now want to illustrate some of these dynamics through consideration of a current phenomenon intimately associated with political correctness: microaggression.

Some Considerations Concerning Microaggression

I came upon the concept of microaggression fairly recently, in reference to unintentional slights, admittedly micro, of a racial nature. At first, I thought it was a parody, but it turned out my students had known about it for quite some time and took it very seriously.

Going to the web to discover the breadth of my ignorance, I learned that it was vast. Googling "microaggression" revealed articles in many major periodicals as well as an enormous number of blogs, many of which contained testimonials of occasions of microaggression that seemed to be effectively infinite. A story in the *Times* (Vega 2014) told me that a blog started in 2010 by two Columbia University students, as part of their Microaggression Project, had received more than 15,000 submissions and over 2.5 million page views from 40 countries.

I found out that the term originated with a professor of psychology and education named Chester M. Pearce in 1977. It was popularized by a Chinese-American professor of psychology named Derald Wing Sue, beginning in 2007, who then followed with numerous books and articles, most notably a book called *Microaggression in Everyday Life: Race, Gender, and Sexual Orientation* (2010), which is summarized in a contemporaneous piece with the same title in *Psychology Today* (Sue and Rivera 2010), from which these passages are taken.

As Sue and Rivera define it:

> Racial microaggressions are the brief and everyday slights, insults, indignities and denigrating messages sent to people of color by well-intentioned White people who are unaware of the hidden messages being communicated. … Our research and those of many social psychologists suggest that most people … harbor unconscious biases and prejudices that leak out in many interpersonal situations and decision points. … Getting perpetrators to realize that they are acting in a biased manner is a monumental task because (a) on a conscious level they see themselves as fair minded individuals who would never consciously discriminate, (b) they are genuinely not aware of their biases, and (c) their self image of being "a good moral human being" is assailed if they realize and acknowledge that they possess biased thoughts, attitudes and feelings that harm people of color.

The idea here is that, because of social pressure, overt, conscious racism has become unacceptable, but it has not disappeared. It has gone underground. Where the social pressure came from that forced the racist, white supremacist society to drive its defining characteristics underground is not explained, but the argument is that it has been maintained; it provides great benefits to whites, called "white privilege," and white people have been marinated in it. They cannot escape, and they inevitably succumb. As a result, they are just as racist as they were before; they just don't know it. In fact, in many ways, the situation is worse than it was before. He asserts that many scholars believe that overt bigotry is easier for victims to deal with than the subtle and unintentional forms, since there is no guesswork involved. It is the latter that create the overwhelming problems.

Now, it is easy enough to see that there may be a problem here. Communication requires that a message be both sent and received; and it must be the same message. According to Sue, "people of color," as well as persons of other marginalized groups, feel that they are receiving those messages on a more or less constant basis. But have the messages they think they have received been actually sent by those they think have sent them? If not, our question immediately turns to the state of mind of the receiver, and the psychodynamics of interpretation that have led to the experience of being demeaned.

The implication here is that Sue has access to the unconscious of those presumed to send these messages, whom Sue calls the perpetrators, and can read it unerringly, as can every other member of a marginalized group. In his book, he offers dozens of examples of such reading, all based on anecdotes, offering no proof of their validity in any case.

In some cases, the interpretations seem reasonable enough, but it is difficult to believe the anecdotes have been faithfully reported. For example, he reports the case of a lesbian client who reported her orientation to a straight male therapist by saying that she was "into women." The therapist claimed he was not shocked by this disclosure since he had a client once who was "into dogs." (2010, p. 14)

Often, the anecdotes are believable, but the interpretations are forced. For example, he is invited by an Ivy League university to conduct a diversity training program "related to making the university a more welcoming place for students, staff, and faculty of color." Giving a presentation to a meeting of the Deans of all the colleges, he observes that all are white and that women are "underrepresented." Remarking on this he asks, "Do you know the message you are sending to me and other people of color on this campus?" And then he spells it out. Students and "faculty of color" receive the message that they and their kind are not welcome at the university, that they will not feel comfortable if they choose to come, and that if they choose to stay they will be limited in their capacity to advance. Students will not graduate and faculty will not get promoted nor granted tenure. (2010, p. 25)

Why a university administration hostile to "people of color" would lavish its resources on trying to welcome them is not explained.

Another such strained interpretation is made when a third-generation Asian American was complimented by a taxi driver for speaking such good English. From this, he draws the message that Asian Americans are "perceived as perpetual aliens" in their own country and not "real Americans." Thus, the voice of a cab driver—a profession that, in my experience, is dominated by immigrants—is being taken here as conveying some kind of authoritative view on who is and who is not a "real American." (Sue and Rivera 2010)

It is difficult to avoid the impression that, more often than not, rather than discovering a hidden message in the anecdotes, Sue begins with the message, selects or crafts an anecdote in which to find it, and then pronounces "Ahah, there's another one." The process is not discovery, but the advancement of a political point. A degree of distortion is generally involved.

Deconstructing the various modalities of this distortion would take a book easily the length of Sue's, but one may be useful for the purpose of illustration. What the political point is, and how the distortion of anecdote/interpretation furthers it, will be returned to presently.

This anecdote/interpretation is a favorite of Sue's, who discusses it extensively in several places. I quote the whole thing as it appears in the *Psychology Today* article:

> Not too long ago, I (Asian American) boarded a small plane with an African American colleague in the early hours of the morning. As there were few passengers, the flight attendant told us to sit anywhere, so we choose *[sic]* seats near the front of the plane and across the aisle from one another.
>
> At the last minute, three White men entered the plane and took seats in front of us. Just before takeoff, the flight attendant, who is White, asked if we would mind moving to the back of the aircraft to better balance the plane's weight. We grudgingly complied but felt singled out as passengers of color in being told to "move to the back of the bus." When we expressed these feelings to the attendant, she indignantly denied the charge, became defensive, stated that her intent was to ensure the flight's safety, and wanted to give us some privacy.

> Since we had entered the plane first, I asked why she did not ask the White men to move instead of us. She became indignant, stated that we had misunderstood her intentions, claimed she did not see "color," suggested that we were being "oversensitive," and refused to talk about the matter any further. (Sue and Rivera 2010)

They ask whether this interpretation represented hypersensitivity, noting that this sort of question is one that black people are faced with all the time in their everyday transactions with well-meaning white people. But this caution is for rhetorical effect. He shows no sign whatever that he is in any doubt. The flight attendant harbored prejudice toward him, he is certain.

In the *Psychology Today* article and elsewhere, Sue is explicit that he took the attendant's request personally, seeing it addressed specifically, even if not exclusively, to his Chinese-American self. There is no indication that his discomfort arose from empathy with his African-American colleague, or that he believed her victimhood was in any way different from his own. His feeling for her was, apparently, solidarity as another person "of color."

What is striking here is the length Sue goes to find himself victimized in this situation. He accuses the attendant of having singled them out "as passengers of color ... told to 'move to the back of the bus.'" The reference here was obviously to the segregationist practice of forcing black people to sit at the back of the bus. But that practice, which had only been the custom in the deep American South and disappeared with the Public Accommodations Act of 1964, applied only to African Americans, not to people of Chinese descent.

Not only were Chinese-Americans not required to sit at the back of Southern buses, but their history had no similarity whatever to the history of American blacks. They were not brought here as slaves, they were not subject to being lynched, they were not segregated into atrocious schools and lousy housing, not forced to drink at separate drinking fountains or forbidden to eat at restaurants, and so on. Wing tries to gloss over this dissimilarity with the designation "people of color," but this is a political term that arose within the identity politics of the recent past and relates to no historical reality. Not only are their histories entirely different, but present day attitudes toward them are also entirely different. Sue wants to unite these groups "of color" by claiming their equal victimization as inferiors oppressed by the unanimously held belief by whites in their racial supremacy, but his exertions in this regard are contradicted by almost every comparison between these groups that he makes.

For example:

> Asian American students may be labeled shy, inhibited and repressed because their cultural dictates emphasize subtlety, and indirectness in approaching tasks. Communication styles of African Americans, because they emphasize passion, may be viewed as "out of control and too emotional." (Sue, 2010, p.78)

How it can be that ascriptions of shyness and law abidingness connote inferiority is not explained. And then there is this:

> Ascription of Intelligence—This microinsult is usually related to aspects of intellect, competence, and capabilities. Saying "You are a credit to your race" contains an insulting metacommunication ("People of color are generally not as intelligent as Whites.") … The belief that African Americans are intellectually inferior is quite a common microaggression.

But:

> when White students ask Asian Americans for help on their math/science problems (Asians are naturally good at math.), ascription of intelligence may be in operation (*ibid*, p.35).

There are other "microaggressions" that Asians are subjected to: their women are "exoticized," they are told they speak good English, or asked where they were born, or told that they are a "model minority" in terms of their economic progress, and so on. None of these will get Sue anywhere near the back of the airplane.

There is another such contrast that deserves special attention.

> Criminality/Assumption of Criminal Status—The theme of this microinsult appears to be very race specific and relates to beliefs that a person of color is presumed to be dangerous, potentially a criminal, likely to break the law, or antisocial. Numerous examples of this apply to African Americans and Latinos. Interestingly, our studies suggest that assumption of criminal status is seldom attributed to Asian Americans. Indeed, they are often viewed as law abiding, conforming, unlikely to rock the boat, and less prone to violence (*ibid*, p.35)

Here again, it is difficult to see how law abidingness can be seen as inferiority. Beyond that, though, it is interesting that Sue finds it "interesting" that the assumption of criminal status is attributed more frequently to African Americans than to Asian Americans, since by all measures the former are far more likely to commit crimes than the latter. For example, FBI Uniform Crime Reports record that, in 2013, blacks committed about 28.3 % of the crime in the USA, including 52.2 % of murders and non-negligent homicides, and 38.7 % of violent crimes; this though they represent only about 13 % of the US population. Asians, by contrast, committed 1.2 % of the crime, though they represented about 5 % of the US population. (FBI 2015)

For Sue to find this interesting suggests he is unaware of it. But the disproportionate level of criminality among African Americans is hardly a secret, and it is hard to understand that anyone who undertakes the study of race does not know it. Evidently there is a bit of solipsism here. Microaggressions seem to exist in a world by themselves, without connections to facts. They are statements, or beliefs, whose falsity is taken for granted, though it has nothing to do with evidence.

The issue this raises concerns the way Sue's mind is working when he makes a charge of microaggression. Consider the case of the flight attendant in this connection. We cannot know her attitude, but neither could Sue. His attribution of a racist attitude that would encompass both groups is absurd. Yet this attribution is made with such confidence that the attendant's denial is taken as evidence of what she denies; indeed as a microaggression in its own right. And the possibility that there might have been other reasons for her choice, for example, that it was by chance or with the intention of inconveniencing two people instead of three, are not even considered.

So the issue shifts from the attendant's mind to Sue's. What was there that led him to believe that she was being racist toward him, in a circumstance where she almost certainly was not? This is the point at which the theory of anti-Oedipal politics and the normalization of pristine self come back into operation.

I will turn to that shortly, and also the question of why people buy into this program, but first I want to get beyond the limits set by Sue's, perhaps idiosyncratic, perspective and look more widely into the question of how the term microaggression is popularly used.

Microaggression in Common Usage

To that end, I turned to some of the paradigmatic locations on the web, specifically *BuzzFeed: 21 Racial Microaggressions You Hear On A Daily Basis* (2014) and Microaggressions: Power, Privilege, and Everyday Life

(2014) where people have posted their stories of the microaggressions committed against them. I'll refer to these as BF and MI, respectively. Below are some entries that seem to me exemplary.

First is my absolute favorite, on a blog where people post examples of racial microaggressions:

> Was biking through town when two women yelled "Konichiwa!" at me … I'm Vietnamese. And I was born in California.(Also, where's the female solidarity?) (MI)

Recognizing the term *konichiwa* as Japanese, I looked up the definition. I assume that, if she also did not know what it meant, she looked it up also. It means "Good afternoon." Now, how can being addressed with "Good afternoon" be considered an act of aggression?

There are two components to this. One is that these women "yelled" this at her, perhaps indicating over-familiarity; but how would that be racial? She might think of it as racial if she thought that their perception of her race was what inclined them to over-familiarity. But the issue in her mind seems to be their mistake about her race. And that would not be relevant to a racial cause of their over-familiarity.

It seems that the racial part is that she is Vietnamese, and American born, but was addressed in Japanese. They were presuming that she would understand the Japanese word, even though she was Vietnamese and born in the USA.

That this was experienced as an aggression can only mean that they were supposed to know that she was Vietnamese, and possibly even that she was born in America. In other words, the presumption was that they should have known who she was. And that it was an act of aggression against her that they did not.

And they were supposed to know this without asking. Asking where a person is from is a paradigmatic microaggression, supposedly conveying the charge that the person being asked does not belong here. (Sue, p. 34)

The presumption that others would know who one is runs through many of the entries, and is often accompanied by the belief that not knowing who one is sends a message that massively undermines one's identity.

> *Stranger:* What do you do?
> *Me:* I'm a professor.
> *Stranger:* You're way too young to be a professor. You look like a student.

I'm in my 30s and I dress more professionally than my colleagues. But I'm also petite and female. My male partner, who has the same age and occupation, is never told that he doesn't look like a professor. It sends me the message that I'm an imposter, merely play-acting at being a serious scholar or authority figure. Made me feel like no one will take me seriously despite my accomplishments. (MI)

This may happen even when the message comes from someone whose stupidity and rudeness are evident, and would ordinarily be grounds for not taking their views seriously: For example,

I work in a Mexican restaurant. My white male coworker is serving a table when he turns around and asks me: "Hey, you're Mexican, how do you pronounce this word in Spanish?"

I reply: "I'm not Mexican, I'm Paraguayan."

He proceeds to say loudly: "No one cares, it's the same damn thing."

This was said right in front of our costumers. (*sic*) Not all Latinos are Mexican and Mexicans are not similar to Paraguayans. I felt belittled by the fact that my entire history, people and culture can be dismissed by one ignorant comment. (MI)

Most important, others are supposed to know how one defines oneself. For example:

"What are you?"
HUMAN
Being bi-racial doesn't make me a what. (BF)

Or:

My black friends: You aren't really black though, you act like a white girl.

My white friends: You aren't really white though, you're like dark.

All of them telling me I have to be one, I can't be both. I'm just me though. Makes me feel like I can only be a certain race if I look and act a certain way. (MI)

And they are supposed to feel about you, typically expressed through their speech, in a way that conforms to your self-definition.

While practicing my martial art (Aikido) my partner, a large and muscular middle-aged man, begins to instruct me as if he is doing me a favor—

despite the fact that we aren't too many ranks apart and he has no teaching certification.

I felt worthless, as if his status as older, stronger, and a man gave him the right to break dojo etiquette (only instructors should instruct) simply because of my small, girl status. His intentions were good, but his actions so incredibly misguided, unhelpful, and condescending. I felt as though I couldn't say anything without sounding like an overly sensitive little girl (MI).

Starbucks employee (male): What can I get you Sir?
Me (transitioning female to male): [order]
SE: Oh I'm sorry Miss.
Me: Uh … it's sir.
SE: Here's your coffee MISS sorry again MISS.
My friend thinks I "confused" him. I'm also a college student so if I wasn't sir, I should have at least have been ma'am. (MI)

"When are you going to have some kids? You know you're not getting any younger." This is what a co-worker said to me after learning that someone we both know is expecting a child. What if I can't have children? What if I don't want children? Why don't people think about that before speaking? (MI)

Just because I'm Mexican, that doesn't mean I should be the automatic first choice for the role of Dora the Explorer in the high school skit. (BF)

This sensitivity is demanded even from people who don't know that you are there and listening. Evidently, even without knowing you, they are supposed to have you always in mind:

While whale watching on a touristy boat in Maine, we were having trouble getting close to a whale who kept diving farther away from us. I was standing at the very front of the boat and overheard this exchange between two strangers:

Man #1: The whale keeps diving away from us and getting farther out. (laughs) It probably thinks we want to mate with it.

Man #2: It's definitely a female whale, then. It's like, "Get away from me, please, get away from me!"

(They both laugh and Man #2 continues to say things such as, "Get away from me! Stop coming close!" in a high pitched, feminine voice)

I am a 20-year-old sexual assault survivor. I felt shocked, worthless, depressed. (MI)

To sum it all up, and I really do mean all of it, individuals see themselves as being microaggressed against when an interaction does not support their feelings of goodness and importance. In our terms, it does not support the pristine self. The basis upon which one feels good and important is never defended, or even mentioned, but is assumed to be understood and its validity self-evident. They feel violated when there is a lack of support, which means that they expect such support and feel entitled to it, even when as is typically the case, there is no reason to suppose that others have any basis for insight into the way one feels about oneself.

To explain all this, including the attributions made by Sue, we may return to political correctness, anti-Oedipal politics, and the concept of the pristine self.

Political correctness, anti-Oedipal psychology, makes a claim for the love of the mother, which has been stolen by the father. The father is represented here by objective self-consciousness, which was the instrument of his theft. The consequence must be that political correctness is the repudiation of objective self-consciousness. With that, goes the capacity for realistic psychology; anti-Oedipal psychology precludes the possibility of understanding oneself as just another self.

The connection with paranoia here is obvious, but we can take this further. What is critical, in this connection, is that this psychology rules out the understanding that all people are wrapped up in themselves in exactly the same way we are. We lose the capacity to understand that what somebody says generally refers to them, and not to us. It has meaning for them in the way that *they* define meaning; it supports them, not us. Assuming that we are entitled to be their center of self-reference is absurd and makes no more sense than their assuming that we are the centers of meaning for them.

The mother is the guarantor of the pristine self, which the rise of political correctness has normalized. The pristine self is the self conceived as again fused with the primordial mother, loving and omnipotent. Her love means the validation of our narcissistic belief in our importance and goodness. Such a person would feel themselves entitled to being the center of a loving world. As a result, everything becomes personal. And when the personal reference is not maternal love, as is usually the case, it has to be experienced as hateful.

This would mean that whatever we do would be worthy of love, hence justified, since we do it. In the absence of objective self-consciousness, which could provide an independent source of validation, our thoughts and feelings are correct and valid since we, under the aegis of mother, are the center of meaning; our thoughts and feelings *define* reality.

This is what stands out most of all in these stories of microaggression. They all represent self-contained moral universes that have been invaded by alien beings, but who just turn out to be other people. My dominant reaction to them is the desire to say "this isn't about you."

The outsize reaction one often sees, in which someone feels massively invalidated by a stupid or childish remark arises from this lack of objective self-consciousness, from fusion, and from the idea of fusion as the norm. Fusion would leave the person entirely open to the outside, and without defenses. Such a person, so to speak, would have no filters. Comments from others would go directly to the core of their being.

I do not know what proportion of people is afflicted with this boundary loss. For our purposes, though, the idea that fusion is normal, what I call the normalization of the pristine self, and that impingement on one's sensibilities represents a violation of one's self, would serve the same purpose of explanation. In either case, people lose the capacity to say of somebody's stupid and insensitive remark, whether directed to them personally or not, "That guy is just a schmuck and what he says is not to be taken seriously." What has been lost, in other words, is the definition of the word "schmuck."

The result of all this is that the frictions of human life, the impingements on our narcissism that the existence of other minds makes inevitable, have come to seem intolerable. This is equally true about the organization of minds to form a common frame of reference, which is and always will be the cornerstone of civilization. This will have an obvious bearing on the capacity of a society to generate and sustain social capital.

At this point, we need to note that nothing within the dynamics I have discussed so far is specific to race. But the whole issue we have here, especially in the blogs, supposedly concerns "racial" microaggression, and it is apparent that racial issues have been the paradigm through which other issues of "oppression" have been defined. The question I now want to address is where race comes into the picture, and therefore what that paradigm means.

The feeling that an impingement is due to race, or some other aspect of identity, is not, as Sue's flight attendant illustrates, and as Sue directly concedes, necessarily related to some feeling in the aggressor, at least any conscious feeling.

The view I want to propose is that, for those who make accusations of racial microaggression, race represents the basis upon which claims for the violation of one's pristine self can be asserted. Sue's idea of his race, for example, was simply himself written large. Since he is of a certain race, he is in a position to claim that any impingement on his pristine self is directed at him because of that race. In this way, he can transform any friction with impersonality into a racial microaggression against himself.

This puts him into a position that is much more politically advantageous, and he can use that to define the situation in a way that augments the power of that definition.

It is of great interest, in this regard, to consider the sheer tendentiousness of his claim that the flight attendant was being racist toward him. Making the claim on behalf of his Asian self would have lacked serious credibility, so he mobilized the concept of the "person of color," eliding the difference with African Americans, where a much more powerful narrative was available. In doing so, he sought to mobilize their narrative to amplify his influence in this situation and, through his various recountings, in the world.

But to what end? Recall that the premise there was that the father had deprived us of the love to which we were entitled. So the power here is a moral power, consisting of two parts. First is a demand for the maternal love, to which we are entitled as result of the father's theft. This takes the form of being validated in one's narcissism, and therefore one's feelings and perspective. In effect, this is the power to define the situation. This would be an expression of mother's love, but takes place only in the absence of objective self-consciousness, which as we know is the province of the father. That is the second form the power employed through political correctness takes. It is the power of destroying the father.

Race, therefore, is the ground upon which one claims the right to such support. It provides a narrative, into which one may fit oneself, of the perfidy of the father. Generally, this is expressed on one's own behalf, but it can also be experienced vicariously, on behalf of those with whom one identifies. A related dynamic involves an expansion of one's race to include others whose claim to victimization is regarded as strong, so that the combined "race" can assert a more powerful claim. This is what is behind Sue's use of the term "people of color."

The difficulties this would cause for social association are self-evident. The narcissism here is obvious, and the problems arising from the narcissists' requirement to have others' lives revolve around their own are well known. When this narcissism is defined as the core of moral order, the demands upon others will be asserted with a feeling of righteousness, which will be particularly problematic when it is in opposition to the righteousness of other groups who are asserting their own narcissistic claims on their own behalf. Such associations cannot help but be unstable and unappealing, except to the extent that individuals can identify with each other based on their feeling of being jointly abused by an outside villain, whose villainy consist in the refusal to support the self-definitions and self-feelings that the victims have in common. So the villains get to be called racist, or sexist, or whatever fits. In other words, political groups directed against the same villains are likely to be the only kind of associations experienced as tolerable and all of the social interest that such people have will be channeled into them. For many, it will be their only interest and concern, aside from themselves, of course, but even that concern is likely to be defined in terms of their politics.

Another aspect of this arises from the fact that objective self-consciousness will be under sustained attack; the paternal function and its role in society will be increasingly attenuated. But it is through objective self-consciousness that society organizes itself. That means that organization will become increasingly problematic. This will take place at every level and every manifestation of social capital, aside from the political.

Sue, in fact, makes clear what the scope of his critique comprehends. All of our institutions are expressions of white supremacy, and therefore of racism, and must be rejected. This becomes manifest when there is a conflict between social norms and the self-expressions of racial minorities or other "marginalized" groups. Sue says, with regard to African-Americans, that conformity to white standards in various social and work settings and being concerned with the consequences of violating norms or letting one's feelings be known often results in emotional turmoil. Under these circumstances, black people can feel like cowards or sell-outs, resulting in a loss of integrity. (2010, p. 81)

This rules out the defense of a norm on the basis of a social function that it serves. The only issue for preferring one norm over another is group identification. It is, therefore, a microaggression for a white, or for that matter anyone who identifies with the social order, to stand in defense of the norms into which they have been socialized and to offer reasons why they would be preferable to the group expressions that conflict with them.

The central political fact of our time is that the father, standing here as the embodiment of the society, is being repudiated, not identified with.

His achievements have been denigrated; all that is identified with him are the features that are found objectionable. The psychological ground for the rejection of these charges of racism, which, as Sue says, are not consciously recognized in the self, are therefore not available. Accusations supported by nothing more than the feelings of the accuser, no matter how spurious and paranoid, in the absence of a positive feeling of one's identity on the part of the accused, lay waste to anything before them.

The fact that there cannot be grounds for defending norms that are under attack means that grounds for defending them cannot be legitimate even when they are not under attack. With one exception, therefore, no basis for association can be sound. That exception arises from the premise upon which this revaluation of norms takes place: the political association of anti-racism.

This is what Putnam found.

What the paternal function accomplishes, the creation of social order based on mutual comprehensibility, or in Putnam's terms social capital based on trust, the doctrine of microaggression, playing out the anti-Oedipal dynamics of political correctness, undoes. A world that is centered around every one of us has no center at all, and it is hard to see how it can even be called a world, as opposed to an essentially infinite set of mutually incomprehensible and antagonistic microcosms.

Within these circumstances, our entire social inheritance is in terrible peril. New groups develop their existence *against* the old, which in this case would refer to anything that already exists. What exists cannot make a case for itself, whether there is a case to be made or not. Any case that could be made would be experienced as microaggression by the others. Culture would be redefined as an attack upon itself.

Conclusion: The Good Father and the Bad Father

The recognition and adoption of the paternal function gave birth to the idea of what a father should do and be. The primal father acted only on his whim. He recognized no subordinacy to a role or to rules or norms; there was nothing he felt he had to do. Through the organic act, fatherhood was defined in terms of its function, as a locus of rights, obligations, and responsibilities. My claim is that it was the breakdown of the paternal function that Putnam picked up in his survey, and that has been caused by the anti-Oedipal psychology that underlies political correctness. This cannot help but have consequences.

Reflecting on the *pax romana*, Edward Gibbon (1909) said:

> If a man were called to fix the period in the history of the world, during which the condition of the human race was most happy and prosperous, he would, without hesitation, name that which elapsed from the death of Domitian to the accession of Commodus. The vast extent of the Roman empire was governed by absolute power, under the guidance of virtue and wisdom. The armies were restrained by the firm but gentle hand of four successive emperors, whose characters and authority commanded involuntary respect. The forms of the civil administration were carefully preserved by Nerva, Trajan, Hadrian, and the Antonines, who delighted in the image of liberty, and were pleased with considering themselves as the accountable ministers of the laws. Such princes deserved the honor of restoring the republic, had the Romans of their days been capable of enjoying a rational freedom.

With Nerva to the Antonines, we have the good father. As the bad father, we have Domitian and Commodus. The difference between them was that the good fathers *carefully preserved the forms of civil administration* ... and *were pleased with considering themselves as the accountable ministers of the laws*. In other words, the good fathers defined their roles through the paternal function and subordinated themselves to their function, while the bad fathers did not. The bad fathers took the power of the emperor, which the good fathers had in equal measure, and used it to support their whim.

We have seen this before, in the difference between the primal father, who held himself accountable to nothing and no one, and the sons, who defined their role as acting *in the name of the father*, in accordance with *the function of the father*; as the father *should have* acted.

There is a certain orgiastic quality to the assault upon the father. It seems to be assumed that something good will happen when he is destroyed. But that idea comes from internal causes, not realistic external appraisal.

The destruction of the good father leads to freedom only for an instant. After that, something moves in to fill the vacuum. In the absence of a supporting idea of the good father, it is likely to be the primal father *redux*, the bad father, the tyrant.

I end with another well-known quotation, this one from Robert Bolt's (1962) play about Sir Thomas More, *A Man For All Seasons*:

Roper: So now you'd give the Devil benefit of law!
More: Yes. What would you do? Cut a great road through the law to get after the Devil?
Roper: I'd cut down every law in England to do that!
More: Oh? And when the last law was down, and the Devil turned round on you—where would you hide, Roper, the laws all being flat? This country's planted thick with laws from coast to coast—man's laws, not God's—and if you cut them down—and you're just the man to do it—d'you really think you could stand upright in the winds that would blow then? Yes, I'd give the Devil benefit of law, for my own safety's sake.

Notes

1. The only occasion I know where he tries to explain this disturbing phenomenon was in an interview with Michelle Martin on National Public Radio (2007), where she asked how he could explain his findings concerning the breakdown of in-group trust.

   > Prof. PUTNAM: Well, I don't know for sure, actually. It's an interesting puzzle. I think part of it is that when we're around a lot of people who we don't know very well and whose cultural backgrounds and moves we don't know very well, we don't know quite how to read anybody. So we don't know if when somebody looks at us, you know, square on, does that mean hi, glad to have you here, or does that mean get out of my way?

   But notice that this explanation does not specifically address the question that was asked, and that it is, at any rate, questionable in its own right. Being among people who are different should not diminish our solidarity with people who are in some way like us, but enhance it. Try this thought experiment: Ask yourself where a New Yorker would be more likely to start a conversation with a Michigander, at a party in Chicago or at one in Beijing?
2. When this validation takes place in the realm of artistic expression, we refer to this maternal figure as the muse.

References

Bolt, Robert. 1962. *A Man for All Seasons*. New York: Vintage.
BuzzFeed. 2014. 21 Racial Microaggressions You Hear on a Daily Basis. http://www.buzzfeed.com/hnigatu/racial-microagressions-you-hear-on-a-daily-basis#.duM6kdbK56.

FBI Crime in the United States 2013. 2015. https://www.fbi.gov/about-us/cjis/ucr/crime-in-the-u.s/2013/crime-in-the-u.s.-2013/tables/table-43.

Freud, Sigmund. 1911. *Psychoanalytic Notes on and Autobiographical Account of a Case of Paranoia (Dementia Paranoides)*, Standard edn., vol. 12. London: Hogarth.

Freud, Sigmund. 1917. *Introductory Lectures on Psychoanalysis*. London: Hogarth.

Freud, Sigmund. 1922b. *Some Neurotic Mechanisms in Jealousy. Paranoia and Homosexuality. The Complete Works of Sigmund Freud*. London: Hogarth.

Gibbon, Edward. 1909. *The History of the Decline and Fall of the Roman Empire*. Vol. 1. London: Methuen.

Goldsmith, William. 2006. Prof. Disputes Paper's Portrayal. *Harvard Crimson*, October 26.

Lacan, Jacques. 1993. *The Seminar. Book III. The Psychoses, 1955–56*. Trans. Russell Grigg. London: Routledge, p. 268.

Lloyd, John. 2006. Study Paints Bleak Picture of Ethnic Diversity. *Financial Times*, October 6.

Martin, Michel. 2007. Political Scientist: Does Diversity Really Work? *Tell Me More. National Public Radio*, August 15.

Microaggressions. 2014. Power, Privilege and Everyday Life. http://www.microaggressions.com/.

Putnam, Robert D. 2007. E Pluribus Unum: Diversity and Community in the Twenty-First Century. The 2006 Johan Skytte Prize Lecture. *Scandinavian Political Studies* 30(2): 137–174.

Richwine, Jason. 2009. A Smart Solution to the Diversity Dilemma. *The American: The Journal of the American Enterprise Institute*, August 12. http://www.aei.org/publication/a-smart-solution-to-the-diversity-dilemma/.

Sue, Derald Wing. 2010. *Microaggression in Everyday Life: Race, Gender, and Sexual Orientation*. New York: Wiley.

Sue, Derald Wing, and David P. Rivera. 2010. Racial Microaggressions in Everyday Life. Is Subtle Bias Harmless. *Psychology Today*. https://www.psychologytoday.com/blog/microaggressions-in-everyday-life/201010/racial-microaggressions-in-everyday-life.

Vega, Tanzina. 2014. Students See Many Slights as Racial "Microaggressions". *New York Times*, March 21.

CHAPTER 4

Analysis of a Racism Hoax at Oberlin College

Writing in a peer-reviewed scientific publication, Sara Winter, a psychologist, says:

> All the white people I know deplore racism. We feel helpless about racial injustice in society, and we don't know what to do about the racism we sense in our own groups and lives. Persons of other races avoid our groups when they accurately sense the racism we don't see (just as gays spot heterosexism in straight groups, and women see chauvinism among men). Few white people socialize or work politically with people of other races, even when our goals are the same. We don't want to be racist—so much of the time we go around trying not to be, by pretending we're not. Yet, white supremacy is basic in American social and economic history, and this racist heritage has been internalized by American white people of all classes. We have all absorbed white racism; pretence (sic) and mystification only compound the problem. (Winter 1977; cited in Sue 2010)

This woman appears to be living in a miasma; a world suffused with racism, which she hates, but which she senses is everywhere, even in the people she knows and herself. This is an experience of the world as polluted and toxic.

Is she correct? Is American society suffused with racism? The prevailing orthodoxy, at least within academia, is that it is. But this is odd, especially since it is uniformly acknowledged that overt racism is extremely

H.S. Schwartz, *Political Correctness and the Destruction of Social Order*, DOI 10.1007/978-3-319-39805-1_4

rare in our time. And Winter herself provides an example of this peculiarity. She and her friends hate racism, she says, and from this I assume we can infer that they are not overtly racist, but racist, it appears to her, they are.

But are they? I propose that they are not. These are the times of political correctness, not of racism. Even demonstrable facts that reflect poorly on racial groups, like the disproportionate involvement of black people in the perpetration of violent crime (FBI 2015), and which, as facts, would seem to be immune from the charge of bias that racism would surely involve, are expunged from the right-thinking mind, let alone spoken.

Is there not racism in this country? I suppose. Not everybody is right-thinking, you know. But the issue is suffusion, and most of those who are not right-thinking are the truly marginal characters. Is there bubonic plague in this country? On the strength of a couple of cases per year in New Mexico, you could say that there is, but that's not something I need to worry about in Jackson Heights.

So what can this racism be? Is it covert? But covert means it cannot be seen. And how can people know that it is there if they cannot see it?

Is it unconscious? That is often said, but when it is said, it is not generally said by people who have very much understanding of the nature of the unconscious. If they did, they would know that when the unconscious expresses itself in behavior, the relationship between the two is never straightforward. For example, it may take the form of reaction formation, in which the behavior that represents the unconscious feeling takes the form of doing the opposite of what the feeling would seem to call for.

I am going to take a different approach to this. I am going to argue that the perception of American society as suffused with racism is not a veridical perception, but a projection. People see it there because they have placed it there.

But would that not again mean that they are racist? After all, if they are projecting it outside themselves, would that not imply that they have it to begin with?

I think not, or at least not in a way that a simple yes or no could comprehend. The issue is far more complex, and certainly far more interesting, than that simple binary can represent. The issue, I suggest, is not a matter of where racism is and how much is there. The question is what do people mean when they say that the world is suffused with racism? What is their experience of being in the world that has led them to say that?

So this is not a question that has an easy answer. I am going to approach it by exploring a series of events that took place a couple of years ago at Oberlin College.

Oberlin Under Siege

Oberlin College is a passionately liberal liberal arts college in Northeast Ohio. Proud of its role as a way station in the Underground Railroad, and of the fact that it was one of the first American colleges to admit black students and to have men and women study together, it was stunned by an efflorescence of racist, anti-Semitic, and anti-gay materials in February, 2013.

This stuff, which was quite nasty, included slurs written on posters celebrating Black History Month, graffiti labeling a water fountain as for whites only, a swastika written on a Science Center window, and various crude flyers. (For some samples, see Jacobson 2013c)

To be sure, there had been incidents of such abuse in the past, but the wave that took place in February seemed to represent a quantum leap.

The level of alarm was high and the response was impressive. Rallies and marches with titles such as "March of Solidarity" and "Stand Up, Sit In" took place. Student groups offered their facilities as places where students could find safety and begin to heal from the pain these assaults had caused them

The abuse seemed to taper off in late February, when, it was later learned, two students who were responsible for at least most of the incidents were apprehended. However, the community reached a new level of alarm on the morning of March 5. Then, a black student named Sunny Tabler driving to Afrikan Heritage House (AHH), her dormitory, sometime before 1:15 AM, saw what she thought was a person in the regalia of the Ku Klux Klan (KKK).

Doubling back to make sure of her sighting, she was unable to confirm it, and her boyfriend, who was driving with her, did not see it. However, upon reaching AHH she reported the incident to her resident assistant, who suggested she call campus Safety and Security. They checked into the matter and did not find anyone in a KKK suit; they did, however, see somebody wrapped in a blanket.

But things were already underway. By 1:30, according to a detailed timeline prepared by some of the students (Students of the Africana Community 2013), the resident assistants had begun awakening their students, who assembled in the dormitory lounge. By 1:45 students from elsewhere on campus had begun to arrive.

Interviewed subsequently on NBC's Today program, a student who was there reported that "It was completely scary. Everyone in that room was like crying, shaking, and they were like completely scared for like the whole night." (NBC News 2013)

At approximately 2:20 AM the Oberlin Police Department arrived and, along with Oberlin Safety and Security, answered questions regarding the investigation of the apparent KKK sighting and other events from the past month.

Eric Estes, the Dean of Students, who had been contacted by a student at 1:26, arrived at 1:40, and was joined at 2:49 by Marvin Krislov, President of the college, whom he had notified. At 5:20, although initially reluctant, in response to student demands and the fact that the Africana Studies Department had canceled classes and called a Teach-In for noon, the administration canceled classes and endorsed the planned gathering.

The Teach-In, called a "Day of Solidarity," was attended by about a thousand students, faculty, and staff, and included the formation of student working groups that would draft proposals for institutional change. It attracted the attention of just about all the news media in the country and support from groups far and wide. Lena Dunham, an alumna and creator of the celebrated television series Girls, tweeted: "Hey Obies, remember the beautiful, inclusive and downright revolutionary history of the place you call home. Protect each other."

Protect each other from what?

The Hoax

An analysis of the Oberlin police files released in August to blogger Chuck Ross at *The Daily Caller* (2013), as a result of a Freedom of Information Act request, revealed that the racist materials disseminated in February had been produced by two students who were acting as "trolls," seeking to get a rise out of the community. As the story developed, especially through the work of William Jacobson at the blog *Legal Insurrection*, it was learned that they were not racists, and in fact one was a well-known campus activist who had worked widely for liberal causes, including the Obama elections. Most interestingly, the college administration had known this by, at latest, February 27, when these students were arrested and, in the presence of college security officials, confessed (Jacobson 2013a, 2013c).Yet, aside from letting on that they believed the incendiary work to have been the product of a small number of students who had been removed from campus, the administration gave no hint that the whole business had been a hoax. They allowed the dominant view of the work as a racist attack to continue and to drive the campus reaction.

The case of the spectral Klansman displays a similar lapse. Let us consider the question of what could possibly have been the purpose of a Klansman, wearing his regalia, (See Note [1]) to walk around the Oberlin College campus at 1:00 on a winter's morning? The regalia, after all, exist for the purpose of intimidation, and to conceal the identity of the individuals taking place in the act of intimidation. But there is nothing intimidating about a single individual walking around a campus at 1 AM. Intimidation would require that the individual make his presence known. But this person was seen only by accident, and clearly did not do anything to create a visible presence. If there was anybody who was threatened, there in the midst of thousands of healthy college students all of whom would regard him as the devil, it would have been the Klansman himself, and he would have been creating this entirely avoidable threat to himself for no conceivable purpose.

Therefore, if the police recognized that a person wearing a blanket would have been close to the description they received, and they knew that there was a person wearing a blanket, then, given the probabilities involved, the presumption had to be that that *was* what it was.

Taking all this together, it is clear enough that the identification of the figure as a student in a blanket was almost certainly correct. Moreover, we have reached this interpretation by a process of analysis that was obvious and by no means arcane. Anyone who was not committed to being credulous could have arrived at it and probably did. But this interpretation, even though it would presumably have prevented a considerable amount of fear and suffering, was not taken into consideration in any substantive way, either by the police or by Krislov and his administration, which was entirely apprised of the situation but allowed it to build into the hysteria leading to the cancelation of classes.

In response to the bloggers' revelation of the hoax, the administration (2013) defended its support for the mobilization through a statement which says, in part:

> These actions were real. The fear and disruption they caused in our community were real ... we draw the line at threats and harassment of any kind. We will not tolerate acts of hatred and threats of violence regardless of motivation.

Jacobson responded that the actions inflicted real pain, to be sure, but that they did so because the students thought they were genuine expressions, rather than a hoax. He likened the situation to someone sounding a fire alarm, and the administration, while knowing that the alarm was a prank, continued to let people believe there was a real fire

So what was going on here? Jacobson's charge was basically that Oberlin's failure was a failure to represent reality. The fear and disruption were contingent upon the students believing that there was real threat. The administration knew that there was not, but didn't tell them. Why not?

I would like to address this question obliquely by suggesting that it did not matter whether Krislov and his administration represented reality in the way that Jacobson and others had in mind. They would not have succeeded in doing so even if they had tried.

The truth is that reality was defined in a quite different way than we are accustomed to seeing and that Krislov had no standing as an authority to represent that reality. In fact, it was defined against him.

Consider this video, which is part of an interview with Krislov broadcast on CNN:

https://www.youtube.com/watch?v=JGwkQCgrLwM (See Note [2])

The back story here is that Krislov's administration was seen as having taken credit for shutting down the college, but he was not entitled to it. This charge was made by a large group of black students and their allies, who claimed he had not responded immediately to their "demand" that the administration shut the campus down, and did so only after they had threatened to blockade the buildings. (Students of the Africana Community, *op. cit.*). He had, after all, arrived at 2:49 AM and had not canceled classes until 5:20. The administration's concern, at the time, that: "cancelling classes ... would be 'giving in' to recent events and would 'disrupt our commitment to learning'" was dismissed.

The disrespect shown to Krislov, and his passivity in the face of this disrespect, are obvious. But even more interesting is what happened afterward.

It appears that there was some feeling, among some students, that Krislov had been treated disgracefully by this group, evidently under the leadership of the Senior Class President, a "trans" person named AD Hogan (personal pronouns "they, them, theirs"), and that this called for a formal apology. The petition provoked a high level of student response. Much of it defined the administration itself as the object of the protest.

Hogan (2013) did not apologize, but claimed, instead, to be appalled by the negative response that the petition represented.

> Students who are not directly targeted by recent events cannot judge nor invalidate the actions of students who are continually marginalized and oppressed, institutionally and interpersonally; instead, we all must listen to the experiences of students of color and queer students and must commit ourselves to allyship when asked to … We all must engage in allyship; allyship means to be committed to actions, accountability, and self-reflection that aim to dismantle structural injustices and daily microaggressions. Allyship requires much more than attending a rally or a convocation and does not include demonizing students who engage in direct action.

Given the choice of whether to oppose or support the disrespect shown to Krislov, it seems that students overwhelmingly chose the latter. I was not able to find any public support for the petition at all, even from those who had signed it.

Characteristic was the response of a student name Megan Bautista (2013), who offered a view of the history. She claimed that Hogan and the other students had been

> respectfully, peacefully, and "properly" addressing the issues of racism, homophobia, anti-Semitism and general bigotry on this campus for years … yet have received little to no recognition from the administration and have made little to no advances.

And, with this as a context, she affirmed her allegiance

> If I had an ounce of the passion that AD had, and if that single ounce was squelched in the fashion that it has been, and if after that a Ku Klux Klansman was spotted walking around my campus and the administration felt that it was not an appropriate cause for immediate action and class cancellation, and if even after all of that the administration made a public appearance to the media that not only completely ignored and diminished my efforts and acted as though my ounce of passion didn't exist and as though they were entirely responsible for any semblance of change and response going on, I would chant "no bull shit" too.

In response to this and many other criticisms, the author of the petition, Emily Robinson, (2013) apologized and groveled. She thanked everyone who had taken the time to share their concerns about the letter. She was surprised, she said:

> I was hearing that people felt that our words were silencing and invalidating their anger, which was not an effect that I expected the letter to have … I did not anticipate how far-reaching the effects of the letter would be.

But she took this as an occasion to learn. She attended workshops and had many conversations with people who felt that the letter attempted to silence their anger, invalidate their feelings, and minimize the importance of the causes they were fighting for. As a result, she came to know better:

> I would like to sincerely apologize to everyone who felt silenced, personally attacked or invalidated in any way by the words that I wrote. I now have a much deeper understanding of why the words were so hurtful, and sincerely regret having harmed any members of our community.

What we can see here, I will argue, is a clash between two definitions of reality. One is the definition which seems most familiar to us. Within this reality, there are a number of objective features that bore upon the state of the college at that point, including whether the threat was real and whether canceling classes would represent "giving in" to the perpetrators. Krislov, by virtue of his formal position as the President of the college, would have been authorized to make a decision based on the full range of those circumstances and his assessment of the ramifications of his decision in the future. But in the other reality Krislov was no figure of authority. This reality was subjective; built entirely out of feelings, especially the feelings of the black students, and objective reality was not an issue. If Krislov did not take orders, he was to be held in contempt.

I suggest that it is in this second idea of reality that we find the idea of the ubiquity of racism. And there can be no doubt about which definition of reality carried the day here.

The question becomes, what are the dynamics of this second idea of reality? I want to offer the framework of anti-Oedipal psychology as a way of understanding this. In doing so, I will show how it is that Krislov had no standing, but had become an object of contempt.

Anti-Oedipal Psychology and Social Justice

As we have seen, anti-Oedipal psychology is built around an identification with an infantile omnipotent image of the mother, who sees the father as inadequate, debased, and contemptible. If he were seen in that way, the idea that the child would identify with and internalize him in order to gain mother's love would fall by the wayside. His image of the father would change entirely.

He could not have earned her love by his accomplishments; vile as he is, he could not have had any accomplishments. He did not earn mother's love at all, but gained it by illegitimate means; in effect he stole it. He took it through fraud or power, or even through the threat of rape or death. Whatever he has done that had previously been thought to have earned him a place in mother's love would come to be seen as a sham and a pretense, a corrupt product, and a waste of resources. They have not been accomplishments of which something positive could be said, but modalities of theft and instruments of oppression.

Since the father's "achievements" have been bogus, we cannot understand the love he has received, directly and indirectly in the form of social approval and accommodation, as being due to his actions, but can only understand it as being vested in his identity, which necessarily embraces those who are like him. This is the root of the concept of *white privilege*.

We can understand, as a corollary, why some have been more loved than others. Channeling the stolen love to himself and those who were like him, which in this case means the heterosexual, white, cis-gendered males, has had the consequence that those who are not like him have been especially deprived. This deprivation is what is referred to as *marginalization*.

Their deprivation, their marginalization, has been a function of a dimension of their identity in which they differ from the oppressive father. This means that in American society where the paradigmatically oppressed group has been African-Americans, objective self-consciousness and social structure, as products of the father, are racist.

As we reconceive the world in this way, social reality is not made out of objective factors such as the division of labor and the structures of exchange, but around moral factors, such as the polarity of racism and oppression, on one hand, and antiracism, which is seen as the pursuit of *social justice*, on the other. Structures of exchange are not objective features of the world; they are the manifestations of the father, which is to say the white, heterosexual, cis-gendered male, and are in no way independent of the way specific groups feel about them.

There is an interesting aspect of this that bears mention. One rarely, if ever, sees "social justice" used in reference to an objective state of affairs; a type of social structure that will be more just than we have now. It is always used as a negation of social injustice. The point is that, linguistically, in the binary social justice/social injustice, the latter term bears the weight of meaning. Social justice is simply the absence of social injustice, and social injustice is simply justice that has been perverted and corrupted by social factors, such as racism. Social justice, then, is a misleading term. In the absence of corruption by social factors, the result is simply justice, the modifier "social" adds nothing to its substantive content. The result of this is to undermine claims about the structural importance of such social factors as racism, which now are asserted to be basic elements of social structure.

In the transformation of objective reality into a manifestation of oppression, we should recall Freud's observation that the paranoid "cannot regard anything in other people as indifferent" and recognize the fundamental dynamic of paranoia, which is projection.

No one can live in society without objective self-consciousness; it is the very premise of language. In order to get rid of objective self-consciousness, we must expel it from ourselves and project it on to something else. The father will do very nicely here, since it is after all the paternal function that is bringing us the news we cannot stand. So instead of hating this news of limitation within ourselves, we will find it in the father, call it racism or whatever, and hate it there.

In this way, we do what projection does. We transform an intra-psychic conflict into an interpersonal one. Instead of tearing ourselves apart, we can, in our fantasy, tear him apart, and emerge from this, again in our fantasy, whole, beautiful, and perfect: the pristine self. We can build a whole world out of this, and each of us can find our place within it, and especially those who have been deprived and marginalized in the past.

We therefore redefine the world as a venue for this struggle, and we redefine ourselves through our roles in this struggle.

Having redefined ourselves in this way, we have made ourselves dependent, for our sense of identity, on the existence and pervasiveness of the racism that we have created through our projection. That is the condition, in which Sara Winter, who wrote our opening paragraph, finds herself.

A critical feature of the world that is defined in terms of this struggle is that it cannot be validated by comparison with external, objective reality, as the world established by the paternal function can. And it cannot be refined by the continual process of responding to feedback that marks the development of objective self-consciousness.

The basic problem here is that this way of seeing things has an irreducible and indispensible fantasy at its core and consists in nothing more than an elaboration of that fantasy.

The father did not steal mother's love. The idea that he did so is based on the proposition that, vile as he is he cannot have had accomplishments. But this vileness is based on a comparison with the perfection of the mother. That is the indispensible premise of all anti-Oedipal psychology. But it is pure fantasy and cannot help but be a fantasy. She is not a real mother, but an infantile image of mother.

In thinking about this, it is useful to enlist Melanie Klein's idea of the good breast. The good breast is the image of the perfect mother, all giving and omnipotent, which is what we are talking about here. But the good breast has a necessary counterpart in the bad breast, who is withholding, terrifying, and dangerous. This differentiation is a product of what Klein calls "splitting," which is a separation of the good aspects of the world from the bad ones. The good breast is made out of all the good aspects of mother, while the bad breast contains all the bad elements. The point is that, for its security, the child needs to believe in mother's pure protective love, so, as a way of maintaining that image of perfection, the contrary experiences with mother are projected into the bad breast.

Generalizing this, we may speak of the good object and the bad object.

Splitting is a feature of what Klein calls the "paranoid-schizoid position," which is to be contrasted with what she calls the "depressive position," a more mature approach to life in which we come to understand that all things have good and bad aspects, and we come to be able to relate to others as "whole objects." Maintaining anti-Oedipal psychology means being stuck in the paranoid–schizoid position and avoiding the recognition that mothers and fathers are, always, whole objects, which is to say real women and real men, with real strengths and real weaknesses.

The idea that the father has had no accomplishments can only arise when what he has done, which has been finite, is compared with the infinite benefices that the idealized mother could have bestowed. Judged against anything finite, for example, when what he has wrought is compared with the features of the world in the past, he has not, it seems to me, done at all badly. And I believe any serious person will come to a similar assessment.

I would think this would be especially true for women. The job that he accepted was to create and expand a space in which she would be safe from the harsh aspects of indifferent, objective reality. Can anyone seriously say he has not made progress in that regard?

Look at just one piece of that. Western women now have the capacity to choose whether and when their sexual relations will result in children, and, if they choose that option, their chances of living through childbirth, and even with a minimum of pain, are excellent, which they were not before, and the chances of their children living through it are excellent as well. Given this, and other things, their overall chances of living their lives into their seventies and eighties, are much, much better than they used to be—actually even better than those of similarly situated men, who are likely to die several years earlier—and they are likely to do so while remaining in possession of most of their teeth, and without lice.

The idea that the father, who stands here as the agent of progress in Western civilization, has not had accomplishments, can occur only in the mind of someone who has never given an instant's thought to the matter. Interestingly, our theory gives us a way of understanding this lapse.

The premise of Oedipal psychology is that we begin with nothing, or at least nothing that is not fantasy. If we are going to have or be anything, we must create it through our efforts. If someone gives us something, without expecting our effort in exchange, it comes from their good will toward us and we should respond with gratitude. The premise of anti-Oedipal psychology is that we begin with everything, and if there is anything that we do not have it is because someone took it away from us. The presence of something good in our lives raises no issue of its origin. Gratitude for beneficence does not come into the equation; its place in the psyche is occupied by resentment for perceived deprivation.

At any rate, since the defining elements of the anti-Oedipal worldview are subjective, it exists only in the mind and loses its existence when it is not being conceived. It therefore can only be kept alive by the continual stimulation of its presence in the mind.

In effect, we are talking about a narrative that is intended to create its own reality through the performance of a drama.

Dimensions of the Drama: Rules of Political Correctness

All of this has dramaturgical implications, which we may think of as basic guidelines for the performance, or rules of political correctness

> Rule One) Hate the father. He is a monster; the bad object. Badness is not a defining feature of what he does, but of who he is. So everything that he does is bad because he does it. Destroy and demistify his works as instrumentalities of his theft of mother's love. This includes, *tout court*, the very idea of objective reality. Given our narcissistic premise, objective reality, is not defined. Indifference is seen as hatred.

This hatred of the father, obviously, must be generalized to the sons of the father; they are "like" him and are the heirs of "white privilege," which they did nothing to earn. They are all guilty of receiving stolen property. The fact that there has been a bait-and-switch here; that they are being charged with not having individually earned advantages that their group collectively created and bestowed, is not generally recognized as a rejoinder. What they are stuck with in their incapacity to identify with their fathers is that they cannot accept, with gratitude, and perhaps with recognition of the ancient injunction that from those to whom much has been given, much will be expected, the fruits of the accomplishments he wrought for their benefit. Rather, they must hate the father, not only for his crimes, but also for depriving them of their innocence.

This also means that they must hate themselves. This self-hatred is not for something that they have done, but is attached to their identity as whites, and especially as white males. They have been stigmatized as white males and their identity has been spoiled, to use Erving Goffman's (1963) phrase.

I have argued elsewhere (Schwartz 2003) that political correctness operates through the dynamics of shame, rather than guilt. This is a case of that. The implication is that they cannot trust themselves to act out of their own spontaneous impulses, including their feelings and immediate perceptions of what is going on around them. These cannot be credited because they are expressions, manifestations, of the despised self. Instead, they believe that they must look to non-white-male others to tell them what the world is about and what their place in it should be. This goes a long way toward explaining their passivity and incapacity to stand up for themselves. They have, in effect, been castrated.

The idea of the father's worth, assertions of the value of what he has created, come to be defined as the ideology of *white supremacy*, expressions of *racism*, and hatred of everybody who is not like him. These define the central tension of the drama: the racism of the father comes under attack by the antiracism of the forces of social justice. This is all, to repeat, taking place in the realm of fantasy.

> Rule Two) The father as bad object has its counterpart in the good object: the mother and those who have been deprived of her love in the past. This group consists those who were not like the father, as defined by race, sex, sexual orientation, or whatever. Collectively, we can call them the oppressed, or marginalized. As the father's badness is a result of who he is, so the goodness of the oppressed is defined by who they are, which is defined by their deprivation at the hands of the father. Those who have been most deprived are most entitled to love and most justified in their hatred of the father.

Oppressed, that is, marginalized, people can, of course, do bad things. But when they do, it is a result of conditions created by the father, and refractions of racism, and so on. They are no less entitled to love for that. Actually, their placement in this tragic position entitles them to even more love.

Interestingly, such people only show up in this drama as those from whom the father has stolen love; in other words as victims. They are not agents, operating to do something. But, as we will see under Rule Four, taken as a claim on mother's love, their victimhood can provide tremendous power. The question is, power to do what? It would seem only to destroy the father. But, then, destroying the father is the route to the ego ideal, in anti-Oedipal politics, so nothing else would be necessary.

In the absence of objective self-consciousness, the structure of the drama is the structure of the world. The structure of the world, that is to say, is redefined through the strength of one's appeal to mother's love on the basis of past deprivation. We must support those who make this claim most strongly in their hatred.

We can see that this is not just a moral imperative. It has ramifications on every level. To begin with, it is a structural necessity. When people speak of "structural racism," we tend to put the emphasis on the "racism," but more important is the "structural" part. In a subjective world like this, defined by its antagonisms, racism/antiracism provides patterning, differentiation, and hierarchy, where there would otherwise be very little.

We can take this a bit farther and bring it back to our original issue: understanding toxicity. Toxicity is a fundamental structural feature of the world defined in this way. Toxicity is the defining feature of whatever is outside of this fantasy of maternal love, which is to say objective reality.

> Rule Three) Celebrate and continually represent to ourselves this mental construct as a way of maintaining our sense of its validity. We must act in accordance with it and demand that others do so as well. Nothing concrete will ever be accomplished in this way, but that does not matter. The concrete is just the father's shtick, and we have deconstructed that. Our political processes here are their own objective. In a very important sense, they give us the only sense of our reality that we have got or can get.

The criticism of our political stance is not tolerable. Since it defines reality, there is nothing outside of it. Hence, there would be no way of defending it by reference to some higher principle. Within our framework, then, criticism can only be understood as action in support of the father, and already an act of hatred and racism. More than anything else, the elaboration, maintenance, and defense of this framework is what is referred to as political correctness.

There is what psychoanalysis calls a secondary gain from this in the form of political identity and the way one sees the meaning of one's life. Adopting a political identity gives us a place in this world; indeed, it is the only acceptable place available.

On one hand, the appeal this political identity offers in the way of heroism is considerable. On the other hand, given the way the pristine self wildly magnifies any threat, the definition of the self in terms of a political identity means that any criticism of one's political framework would actually feel like a threat to one's life. To be sure, this is just a threat to the symbolism of one's life. But the point of psychoanalytic understanding is that symbolism is quite real.

At any rate, this feeling of threat will lead to an intensification of the need to revalidate and celebrate that political orientation.

Political correctness can never sleep. It does not exist except when it is in motion. Therefore, it must always move toward an extreme. No position that can remain stable can be accepted, but must be moved beyond. Any gains that are accomplished can only be seen as transitional, as way stations on the road to a fantasy that, precisely because it is a fantasy, can by definition never be realized.

There is only one currency that can give a sense of where one is and whether one is moving forward. That currency is power. And from this it can be said that gaining and displaying power is the motif that underlies the drama of political correctness in every one of its manifestations.

A final corollary of this is that the issue is never the issue, but is in every case a pretext for creating and developing a movement around it. If this were understood by those responsible for negotiating with the forces of political correctness, it would save them a good deal of heartburn.

> Rule Four) Invoke the love and the power of mother. Rely upon her and have faith that, unencumbered by the father, she will make our lives perfect and ensure that we are touched by nothing but love. This is a proposition that appears only implicitly. It is quite unconscious. But it constitutes our guarantee that we can attack the social order without worrying about the consequences. Everything will be fine. She will take care of us.

Taken together with the previous item, this will have an obvious impact on the place of women, who can much more easily identify with mother and who are more likely to be so identified by others. They can add the rage of those defined as deprived and marginalized because they are different from men, to the power that comes from this identification and create a role with immense strength. Put this together with the submissiveness of men, especially white men, that is a product of all this and it is easy to see that leadership in movements of this sort is likely to be female. This is a falsifiable proposition that can be tested by examining the sex ratio of activists. My claim here is that one will find them to be mostly women.

Political correctness is predominately a feminine project and a manifestation of female power. And this female power is interesting in its own right. We are accustomed to thinking of power in masculine terms, as the feminists tell us; the power of authority, of hierarchy, and so on. But they do not give us a clear-eyed idea of what female power would come down to.

Female power, in this contest, is manifest as the power of taking care of others. Well and good, as far as that goes, except that it helps to explain why people make a point of displaying their wounds and proclaiming their victimhood. We think of victimhood as weakness, but in this case, through its invocation of the power of mother it is a kind of strength.

The problem is that there is no way that this kind of power can be employed in the creation of anything. It is associated, not with success, but with failure; failure is built in as a premise.

That is not to say it has no positive function. How could taking care of those who need it not be positive? The question is where it stands in the whole complex of social life.

Think of this in connection with the opposition between justice and mercy. Both are good and both essential; but while you can have justice without mercy, you cannot have mercy without justice. You can have a rule without exceptions, but you cannot have exceptions without a rule.

At any rate, going back to political correctness as a whole, we can see that an important characteristic of this drama is that it is scalable, so to speak. It will work for an institution in the same way that it works for an individual.

All of this brings us back to Oberlin College.

Oberlin College Redefined

Consider the plight of Oberlin College. The charge against Krislov was that he had not responded immediately to the black students' "demand" that the administration shut the campus down. There is no way of understanding this except that he was not supposed to be in the position of making an independent decision; his authority was not recognized.

Authority, which is to say the right to define reality and decide upon the course of events, had been assigned to the black students (See Note [3]). The responsibility of other students was to be their allies and to support them in their views and feelings and the demands that followed from them. In their perception, Oberlin had been a scene of oppression, in various forms, most notably in the form of racism. The administration had been complicit in its maintenance, and indeed had been its agent.

In this context, the response to the racist actions became an attack upon the college itself, seen as racist, in the name of and deriving its energy from the oppressed. Rachel Berkrot (2013), for example, argued that not only do Oberlin students have a right to call "bullshit," they have an obligation to do so. Oberlin's history is replete with examples of students fighting the administration, on a wide variety of issues, and through a variety of means including sit-ins and building takeovers. Change, she says, has not been brought about by students being polite. So she urges those who were embarrassed by the chants of "no bullshit" to consider that, in so doing, the students were recognizing the bullshit in the institution and calling it out.

> At Oberlin, classes are taught with an almost entirely Eurocentric focus. Most faculty members are white, and students within the classical conservatory are trained to sing and play music like white musicians. These are just some of the ways in which institutional racism manifests itself at this college. This academic institution perpetuates racism and bias because prejudice is ingrained in its very structure.

Of course, this is not to say that this is a problem unique to Oberlin. Systemic racism is everywhere, in her view; it is certainly not a problem only at Oberlin. But, although the administration is getting credit for it, the reason that Oberlin is getting so much attention is that Oberlin's students have chosen to fight it. Fighting institutional racism comes with some unique challenges, including the fact that many white people do not see it. But the students in the CNN protest, she said, were rising to that challenge and should be encouraged in their efforts.

What Berkrot and others are calling for is a redefinition of the college. The purpose of the convocation was to dramatize this redefinition.

Oberlin must become an agency for the pursuit of social justice. Within this redefinition, the default way of understanding Marvin Krislov and his administration would be as the monstrous father. The redefinition of the college would be against him and would repudiate his works. The kind of considerations that, in our customary view of reality, would be seen as the proper domain of the father's authority would be, within the redefined college, seen as anathema.

The structure of exchange is the product of the father. As we understand it, any institution must establish a place within it if it is to survive. But in the redefined world, it is identified with the oppression that the students must fight against.

Commenting on the webcast of the convocation, an anonymous alumna (2013) sets up an opposition between the vitality of the political activists, and the deadliness of the administration, not in terms of their persons, but their function. He says that in his four years at Oberlin:

> we came together many times in the face of hate…
> in these crescendos of terror and hurt, we offer up our passion for each other. we bring powerful testimonies, fierce questions, amazingly moving articulations of bravery and strength.

Again:

> watching the webcast, i reveled in the words of the students and faculty. i am in awe of their brilliance and deeply moved by their words, still echoing for me. as we moved into the q&a, i longed for more shared stories, more ideas and demands.

But when the microphones passed into the hands of an administrator, he cringed. They did not speak the language of liberation. But, then we could not expect them to. Oberlin is a hierarchical institution that is part of the wider, capitalist world and partakes of its oppressiveness.

The result must be that administrators are concerned with many things, and not just the well-being of those who participate in the institution. They are also concerned with things like money and the image or brand of the college. The point we need to recognize is that the college is a business:

> [It] aims to build capital and therefore can't conceive of giving its goods (education, status) away for free. or in exchange for other aid, or simply to create a more dynamic, inclusive, revolutionary, loving, fun, happy world of ideas.

So when Krislov says that the college needs more money in order to get beyond "need-sensitive" admissions:

> what he is saying is that it is not profitable to offer entrance into the institution to those who can't pay. he is stuck, because his obligation to money supercedes any notion of community or generosity.

But it isn't his fault; it comes with the territory:

> his position renders him incapable of aiding the fight for liberation. he will never be able to act for the good of those who are marginalized because his job is to act in accordance with the (white supremacist, heteronormative, money-driven) institution.

This sort of rhetoric is common. The contrary is essentially non-existent. I have seen no recognition of the fact that the college needs to have resources supplied to it by the outside world, which ultimately will not provide such supplies unless it believes it is getting something from the college in exchange. The students' view assimilates exchange to profit making, which is brought about by the white father, doing what he does because that is who he is, and which could be done without if the father could be gotten rid of. The unconscious premise is that the mother will take care of everything.

In all this, we can see that Krislov, whatever he wanted to do, would have been in no position to introduce objective issues related to the institutions survival. Actually, the matter goes to the core of rational consideration itself. Terms like accountability and safety are derided as evasive.

Remember that the drive toward social justice takes place only in the mind. It consists in hatred of the father and love of the oppressed. The convocation was a setting in which this could be instantiated and the psychic reality it represented brought to life. Krislov could not have transformed the situation by revealing that the racist inundation was a hoax, and that the KKK was a student in a blanket. If he had stood in the way, he would just have been rolled over.

The provocations needed to be seen as real in order to legitimatize the response to them, and the students came alive through the response. Nothing could have been allowed to stand in the way of that. They could therefore borrow the reality they needed from the reality of the response. The motive of their perpetration was quite irrelevant.

As I have said, there was no external focus of this action. No program driving forward into concrete behavior was planned. The convocation, by itself, was its own meaning. It is useful, therefore, to think of it as a religious display; a setting for the affirmation of a basic faith; a religious recommitment, rather like a Christian revival. For Krislov to have brought up the hoax would have been seen as the equivalent of a satanic act.

The Convocation as Revival Meeting

Students' appreciation of the event clearly showed that it was appreciated for the feelings it evoked, and the fact that it gave them a chance to acknowledge and separate themselves from their sinfulness, and renew their faith and commitment. A widely circulated piece by Ida Hoequist (2013) reports that she went to the convocation because she wanted to listen, but:

> I came away from it wanting to make visible my support for places and times like that, where POC are lifted up, where those with white privilege recognize that this fight is also theirs because every fight for human rights belongs to every human, and, further, that our place as white people is, for once, not in the spotlight. This one is not about us.
>
> But since I am privileged enough to have been afforded this space to make my voice heard, I will tell you this: I kept going to the events that were organized in response to what happened last night. I marched around Tappan (but really I danced, because that impromptu jazz marching band was mad good). I went to the convocation. I sat in the Finney balcony, clapping in time to the chants (WE ARE O-BER-LIN and TELL ME WHAT COMMUNITY LOOKS LIKE/THIS IS WHAT COMMUNITY LOOKS LIKE and WE ARE FUCKING ANGRY), wondering why the last time I saw Finney that packed was during my freshman orientation, wondering why we students didn't unite like this far more often. I felt togetherness. I felt that solidity again.

I have been unable to find video evidence of the similarity between the Oberlin convocation and a Christian revival meeting, but there is a video available of a similar event that took place at Bowdoin College, another highly acclaimed and expensive liberal arts college in the USA. The motivation for their coming together is about the same, absent the deliberate provocations in the Oberlin case, and the emotional atmosphere, especially in the last two minutes, is what one would expect at a revival: https://www.youtube.com/watch?v=0PsHMioUtTU.

In all of this, courage is a critical component of the students' self-affirmation, because it is the idealization of the self that they affirm. It is central to the project in which they are engaged and can only be understood as defiance of the ubiquitous racism, the toxicity, whose nature we have been trying to understand, and whose cause we have located here. Without it, they, in their own minds, are nothing.

The Vicissitudes of the Pristine Self

The pristine self enters here in important ways. Its premise drives the whole operation. Given that there is very little overt racism, the little racism that there is must go a long way. The case of Maya Mariner (2013) is illustrative.

She was a black student who had been studying in Italy during her senior year of high school. She was hanging out with her Italian friends, when they decided to go down a street where they could see some teenage boys. They made her nervous and she tried to persuade her friends to go in another direction but they kept on going.

> Five seconds after I passed them, I heard "NEGRA!" I turned around and saw the boys smiling. I whipped my head back and walked a few more paces before laughing and saying, "I think they just called me the n-word."

She tried to talk herself out of being disturbed by it, but that did not work. As time went by, she became increasingly depressed. She didn't want to do anything. She didn't want to speak Italian or hang around with Italian friends. She withdrew from participation in classes. Sometimes she would just sit and cry, blaming herself because, if she had only gone down another road, things would have been different; none of this would have happened:

> I was 17, vulnerable in a culture that I didn't know, speaking a language that was unfamiliar. That slur made me realize that even though *I* was so open, and always trying to gain the acceptance of white people, I would never be "one of them."

The second time she was called a nigger was at Oberlin:

> I was out celebrating with a friend because our birthdays were the same week, and while we were going back to our dorms before crossing the street to the Science Center, a passing car came by and I heard "Nigger" as it rushed away. I finished my ice cream, and tried to smile and play it off, but that feeling came back again. Even here in America, my native country, I still did not belong.

What is to be noted here is the disproportionate reaction to these two occasions of mild abuse. The fact, for example, that the first of them was the only occasion of such abuse while she was in Italy does not seem to have been factored into the despair with which she came to color her whole Italian experience.

What needs to be understood here is the fact that in the experience of the pristine self, postulating a boundaryless connection with the world, the unity of the self has its counterpart in the perceived unity of the experienced world. A single insult can translate into the experience of the world as a unified hateful place.

Consider Ida Hoequist again. She says: "I am cisgender and white and pass for straight, but also I am a queer woman and that means I almost never feel both safe and accepted at the same time." This, from a student at Oberlin, where homosexual women are universally celebrated, can only be asserted on the basis of the most stunning distortion and generalization.

Similar considerations apply to the correlative concept of microaggression. In the absence of substantive (macro) aggression, small slights are going to have to suffice for constructing an image of a toxic environment. But small slights are, by definition, small. How is something large going to come out of them?

Part of the answer is that they happen all the time, which is taken to imply that they are structural. The author of the blog *Oberlin Microaggressions* (2013) expresses his intent and vision this way:

> Our blog is primarily for students who have been marginalized at Oberlin. We welcome submissions by marginalized students who wish to speak about their lived experiences.
>
> If you see or hear racist, heterosexist/homophobic, anti-Semitic, classist, ableist, sexist/cissexist speech etc., please submit it to us so that we may demonstrate that these acts are not simply isolated incidents, but rather part of structural inequalities.

The proposition that microaggressions happen all the time and represent systemic features of American society, even including Oberlin College, is common. For example, the February 15 issue of *The Oberlin Review* carried a letter to the editor from the Edmonia Lewis Center for Women and Transgender People (2013), reacting to the racist efflorescence of February.

> We … are acting in solidarity with the Multicultural Resource Center and other student and faculty organizers to address harm caused by racism, queerphobia, anti-Semitism and other forms of structural oppression. … Given our mission statement and commitment to challenging oppression, we are deeply angry and hurt by the recent escalation of anonymous hate speech on campus. While we acknowledge the pain and fear caused by these blatant attacks, we wish to emphasize and bring attention to the microaggressions that individuals face on Oberlin's campus as a part of their daily lives. We must hold each other accountable for condemning visible acts of violence and should think critically about how our daily speech and actions perpetuate these oppressive structures. We acknowledge that these incidents

> are reflective of power dynamics on campus and are by no means "isolated incidents." While Oberlin is known for its progressive politics and commitment to equality, the incidents of the past week are a part of a long legacy of visible and invisible violence toward marginalized communities.

Part of the meaning behind the claim of universal microaggression is the idea that celebrating the classical Western cultural achievements, or for that matter even employing them, is itself a venue for microaggression and, indeed, of white supremacy.

To make this point, I want to return to Sue's discussion of cultural racism as a form of microaggression. He put it this way:

> Cultural racism is perhaps the most insidious and damaging form of racism because it serves as an overarching umbrella under which individual and institutional racism thrives. It is defined as the individual and institutional expression of the superiority of one group's cultural heritage (arts/crafts, history, traditions, language, and values) over another group's, and the power to impose those standards upon other groups (Sue 2010, p. 4).

The basic problem with this is that in any society, virtually everything that is done is a manifestation of the society. For example, in a case that everyone will recognize, the greetings that members of the society offer each other on various holidays take a certain form that is recognized as part of the definition of the holiday: Merry Christmas, for example. Nobody intends that to be a claim of superiority over other cultures, as can be seen in the fact that people offer this greeting among themselves, even with no representatives of other cultures being present physically or even as subjects of discussion.

It may feel that way to others, but as we have seen microaggressions involve projections of aggression that is not there. To get a handle on what this accusation implies we should note that the very language that people speak is a manifestation of the society in exactly the same way. Getting rid of "cultural racism" would mean getting rid of language all together.

The Student Proposals for Institutional Change

As an outgrowth of the mobilization, a number of student working groups were formed to develop proposals for intuitional change. These took their final form in a document submitted in May. (Coalition 2013) For the most part, the students proposed reinforcing the fantasy by deepening and extending the college's political commitments. They make it clear that the assaults of February and March are to be undifferentiated from the panoply of the father's crimes and transgressions:

This is from the introduction to their Final Proposal

> We are not just responding to these recent events; we are addressing the history of racism, cissexism, queerphobia, classism, faith-based discrimination, ableism, sizeism, and eurocentrism in the United States and have a more meaningful discourse on the ways they manifest at Oberlin College and Conservatory. We expect the College and Conservatory to promote social change by validating and affirming all students' voices, especially those whose experiences of exclusion have been marginal to the larger campus discourse.

They then took positions advocating, among other things, the inclusion of a "social justice" framework in all academic coursework, re-evaluating all hiring practices to better promote "diversity," and the placement of the whole educational program in a "larger social context."

Of particular note is that the natural sciences, whose definitional commitment to the importance of objectivity would have made them a last bastion, were brought under attack for their separateness:

> We are disappointed by the Natural Science division's general lack of response to recent hate-based incidents. Physical isolation and racial homogeneity of the Natural Sciences result in an inaccessible community with a limited relationship to other academic departments. Every academic discipline has equal opportunity to identify truths; we must employ this framework to dismantle academic hierarchies.

The specific programmatic remedies included holding a mandatory forum to discuss the various issues of diversity in the natural sciences and modifying courses to include "critical thinking on social issues related to science."

As for the rest, among the key agenda items were mandatory "re-orientation" workshops for students, faculty, and staff led by paid student trainers

The idea that the whole body of the college, including its faculty and staff must be re-educated as a response to, at most, a few instances of racist expression is a fascinating one and takes us back to the way in which Maya

Mariner made a judgment about the racist character of the whole world based on two words uttered by people that she did not know and that did not know her. As I have said, the unitary character of the pristine self leads to seeing the world outside itself in a similarly unitary way.

There may be another way of explaining how it could be believed that a group of people, already among the most politically correct in the world, should *all* be subjected to this "training," but I do not know what it would be.

At any rate, the administration welcomed these proposals and quickly implemented all that it could, making it clear that, as far as was manageable, the rest would be on its continuing agenda.

Summing up the matter, Jacobson (2013b) said:

> Long before the racism hoax in February 2013, Oberlin was a campus heavy with multi-cultural, identity and "social justice" ideologies dominating campus life.
>
> The demands arising out of the bias incidents, encouraged and accepted by the Oberlin administration, pushed that agenda deeper into every aspect of the campus, touching almost every student. While the activists did not get everything they wanted, they got a lot and most important, have regained the momentum they felt they had lost prior to the hoax.

Conclusion

We began with the question of the meaning of the charge that racism is pervasive and turned to Oberlin because, in a well-documented incident, the racism it found so threatening had been manufactured. We noted that the college administration knew it had been manufactured, but allowed the mobilization against it to continue. We asked why the administration did not take the role of authority and provide a reality check.

The answer I have proposed was that reality had been redefined at Oberlin and that, within that redefinition, the charge of racism was, in effect, structural, and had come to provide the meaning of people's college experience and, indeed, of their lives. The fact that the racism had been manufactured in this instance was of no moment. What is more, the structure as it had been redefined was directed against the form of structure within which the administration had authority. The administration had no choice but to go along with the hoax. The hoax represented a deeper truth, within this reality, than anything conferred by the administration's formal position.

But in concentrating on this single incident, we are, in effect, looking at a snapshot, more properly at what amounts to a freeze-frame in an ongoing movie. For the reality at Oberlin is a moving reality. It is defined as progress toward a goal: social justice or whatever one wants to call it. It is precisely because the goal is not only in the future, but also defines the future that relegates objective considerations to secondary importance.

As we have seen, the terms of reference for Oberlin's reality exist only in the mind, and therefore the motion toward the goal of social justice must be continually re-enacted in order to perform its function of structuring people's lives.

Progress in this instance consists in strengthening this way of seeing things in people's minds. This is why progress at Oberlin was defined in terms of increasing the pervasiveness of social justice thematics in all aspects of the college. But this is inseparable from the widening and strengthening of illusion, which had become, in effect, the meaning of the college.

So the question of why the administration went along with the hoax has a deeper answer. It is that the college had, by this point, become itself a hoax, and had dedicated itself to the mission of further hoaxing. In not revealing what they knew about the origin of the racist material, therefore, Krislov and his administration were just doing their job.

But we should not leave without bringing up the question of what is at issue here, and we can do that by referring to a familiar trope that is commonplace among the partisans of social justice. They say that it is a matter of privilege that whites do not have to concern themselves with issues of race; indeed it is a manifestation of their racism.

Another way to look at it, however, is to say that the greatest accomplishment of Western civilization has been the development of objective self-consciousness to the point where it is truly universal and where the tribalisms of race have been left behind. In large measure, we can maneuver in that world, on an equal footing, by accepting its universalistic terms, precisely because we are reasonably confident that others will accept them as well. To the extent than any group cannot so maneuver, the doctrine of objectivity provides us with universalistic ways of correcting such a lapse from principle.

Yet this is exactly what is under attack. And those who have brought it under attack should consider what, in its absence, the alternative can be except for a bottomless pit of ever-increasing toxicity. And those who are in minorities, especially in minorities whose position depends on the good will of powerful others, might at the same time consider that, in the absence of universalistic rules, it is only the winds of political fortune that keep that toxicity from being dumped on them.

Notes

1. A formidable force through several iterations, the Klan has ceased to be a major presence in American society. Today it exists more as a bogey-man than a real threat. The Southern Poverty Law Center says:

   > Since the 1970s the Klan has been greatly weakened by internal conflicts, court cases, a seemingly endless series of splits and government infiltration. While some factions have preserved an openly racist and militant approach, others have tried to enter the mainstream, cloaking their racism as mere "civil rights for whites." Today, the Center estimates that there are between 5000 and 8000 Klan members, split among dozens of different—and often warring—organizations that use the Klan name.

   For a view of where the Klan stands in contemporary American society, check out this video taken at a Klan demonstration and counter-demonstration at the football game between the University of Mississippi and Louisiana State University in 2009: https://www.youtube.com/watch?v=ezkvRywf4vw.
2. The full interview is here: https://www.youtube.com/watch?v=6rMP4NJHmZE.
3. This was clearly the dominant view held by the black Oberlin students, but whether it was unanimous is impossible for me to say. I have seen no evidence of any contrary view, but of course my access to the relevant data is quite limited. An analysis of the relation of black students to this role, and it is certainly a role, would be of great interest, but it will have to wait for another occasion.

References

Anonymous Alumna. 2013. Dear Oberlin. *Oberlin Microaggressions*, March 4. http://obiemicroaggressions.tumblr.com/page/6.

Bautista, Megan. 2013. In Defense of AD Hogan. *Oberlin Microaggressions*, March 7. http://obiemicroaggressions.tumblr.com/post/44766735482/in-defense-of-ad-hogan.

Berkrot, Rachel. 2013. On Examining Roles: The CNN Interview Debate Fearless and Loathing: Oberlin College's Independent Student Website. March 14. Website, formerly at http://www.fearlessandloathing.com is now defunct.

Coalition of Oberlin College and Conservatory Students. 2013. Final Proposal. http://www.docstoc.com/docs/160524391/Oberlin-Student-Proposals-for-Institutional-Change. Docstoc is now defunct. Text is available at Jacobson (2013b).

Edmonia Lewis Center for Women and Transgender People. 2013. *The Oberlin Review*, February 15.

FBI Crime in the United States 2013. 2015. https://www.fbi.gov/about-us/cjis/ucr/crime-in-the-u.s/2013/crime-in-the-u.s.-2013/tables/table-43.

Goffman, Erving. 1963. *Stigma: Notes on the Management of Spoiled Identity.* Englewood Cliffs, NJ: Prentice-Hall.

Hoequist, Ida. 2013. An Open Letter to My Fellow Oberliners. *Oberlin Blogs*, March 4. http://blogs.oberlin.edu/about/activism/an_open_letter_2.shtml.

Hogan A.D. 2013. Apology for Divisive Nature of Responses, Not for Protesting Krislov. *The Oberlin Review*, March 15.

Jacobson, William A. 2013a. The Great Oberlin College Racism Hoax of 2013. August 22. http://legalinsurrection.com/2013/08/the-great-oberlin-college-racism-hoax-of-2013/.

——— 2013b. Oberlin Racism Hoax Exploited to Advance "Even More Extreme Policies". September 1. http://legalinsurrection.com/2013/09/oberlin-racism-hoax-exploited-to-advance-even-more-extreme-policies/.

Jacobson, William A 2013c. Police Release More Records as to Oberlin College Racism Hoax. September 19. http://legalinsurrection.com/2013/09/police-release-more-records-as-to-oberlin-college-racism-hoax/.

Mariner, Maya. 2013. Peace, Love, and Understanding: My Thoughts About the Hate Speech Oberlin College's Independent Student Website. March 6 Website, formerly at http://www.fearlessandloathing.com is now defunct.

NBC News. 2013. Hate Comes to Oberlin. March 5. https://www.youtube.com/watch?v=7CbFbaHGq28.

Oberlin College. 2013. Statement on Bias Incidents. http://news.oberlin.edu/articles/oberlin-college-statement-bias-incidents/#.UhjRJM2S6mc.

Oberlin Microaggressions. 2013. http://obiemicroaggressions.tumblr.com/.

Robinson, Emily. 2013. Letter Requesting Hogan's Apology Reconsidered. *The Oberlin Review*, March 15. http://oberlinreview.org/1957/opinions/letter-requesting-hogans-apology-reconsidered/.

Ross, Chuck. 2013. Meet the Privileged Obama-Supporting White Kids Who Perpetrated Cruel Oberlin Race Hoax. August 22. http://dailycaller.com/2013/08/22/meet-the-privileged-obama-supporting-white-kids-who-perpetrated-cruel-oberlin-race-hoax.

Schwartz, Howard S. 2003. *Revolt of the Primitive: An Inquiry Into the Roots of Political Correctness.* Piscataway, NJ: Transaction Publishers.

Students of the Africana Community, Residents of Afrikan Heritage House, and their (many) Allies. 2013. Oberlin Microaggressions. March 6. http://obiemicroaggressions.tumblr.com/post/44694466981/to-the-oberlin-community.

Sue, Derald Wing. 2010. *Microaggression in Everyday Life: Race, Gender, and Sexual Orientation*. New York: Wiley.

Winter, Sara. 1977. Rooting out Racism. *Issues in Radical Therapy* 17: 24–30.

CHAPTER 5

Anti-Oedipal Dynamics in the Sub-Prime Loan Debacle: The Case of a Study by the Boston Federal Reserve Bank

Like most major disasters, the American sub-prime crisis of 2008 had multiple causes. I will look at only one element of this causal matrix, consisting in some psychological dynamics that led to loans being made to people who, it should have been known, would not be able to pay them back.

My interest here is not in claiming that this dynamic did more than any other to cause the crisis; it is much more limited. The question that interests me is not financial, but psychological. I want to explore why what should have been known was not known. Why were obvious, relevant facts not given their due in financial judgments that turned out to be infelicitous as a result?

My point will be that the psychological configuration within which the loans were made did not recognize, or at least did not take seriously, the kind of information that goes into the calculation of financial risk. Such assessment must be based on an objective analysis of cause and effect, within the context of an agreed framework of rationality. But the psychology within which the loans were made understood their meaning as moral imperatives, and as ends in their own right; the objective analysis of the consequences that would be likely to follow from the granting of the loans was not part of the picture. Moreover, the moralistic analysis gained power because it placed the objective assessment of risk under a moral cloud and made it psychologically insupportable. The irony, of course, is that the moralistic way of seeing things helped to create a situation that,

H.S. Schwartz, *Political Correctness and the Destruction of Social Order*, DOI 10.1007/978-3-319-39805-1_5

even regarding those who were supposed to be the beneficiaries, was catastrophic, economically and morally as well.

My main focus will be on an influential study in the period leading up to the financial crisis, and one whose dynamics are representative of the phenomena I wish to explore. This was a study by the Boston branch of the Federal Reserve Bank that was first reported in 1992 (Munnell et al. 1996). Perhaps more than any other, it was taken as proof that there was racial discrimination in mortgage lending, and it led to a loosening of the criteria used to assess credit worthiness among black mortgage applicants.

The Boston Fed Study

Unlike many previous studies that had reported different rates of loan acceptance by race, this study corrected for standard credit criteria. Using a sample of Boston-area mortgage applications, it found that the standard criteria explained about two-thirds of the difference between white and black/Hispanic rejection rates. Even after this correction, however, minorities seemed to be rejected at a rate of 17 %, as opposed to only 11 % for whites. This difference, they claimed, must be caused by racism. That conclusion was taken by many as a definitive answer to the question.

For instance, an article in the October 9 issue of the *Boston Globe* began its story by saying "A landmark study released yesterday shows that banks in Greater Boston discriminated against black and Hispanic mortgage applicants, offering the most damning evidence to date of racial hurdles facing minority homebuyers." And a story on the same day in the *Wall Street Journal* ran under the headline "Boston Fed finds Racial Discrimination in Mortgage Lending is Still Widespread." (both cited in Sowell 2009).

But as more skeptical analysts quickly found out, the study was seriously and egregiously flawed. For example, Day and Leibowitz (1998) reported that the data were replete with glaring errors.

In some cases, these were errors that should have been noticed by anyone checking over the data, such as negative interest rates. In some cases, the data would have been seen to be erroneous by any economist who was paying attention. For example, a mortgage application that indicated in one variable that the mortgage had been rejected, while another variable indicated that it had been sold on the secondary market, would have to be an error. When Day and Leibowitz ran the analyses with the obvious errors removed, the hypotheses of discrimination were not supported.

Another study found that the results were due to outliers. Forty-nine of the seventy banks under study had rejected no minority applicants at all. Two banks were responsible for over half of the rejections. One of these was a minority-owned bank and the other had an extensive minority outreach program. (Schweitzer 2009, p. 56)

The point to be made here is that the discovery of these errors, which any graduate student would have been trained to spot, and which were rapidly found by outside observers, had no impact on the course of the governmental movement that the study was used to support. It was as if the propelling forces were independent of their presumptive analytic base.

A particularly striking example of this disconnect, at the individual level, was offered in Forbes magazine by Peter Brimelow and Leslie Spencer (1993).

In order to refute the charge that blacks defaulted more, the study intended to take account of comparative default rates. What they found was that there was no relationship between the racial composition of census tracts and the default rates, which indicated to them that black and whites were equally likely to default.

But Brimelow and Spencer, interviewing Alicia H. Munnell, Boston Fed senior vice president and the chief researcher, pointed out that there was a serious flaw in this interpretation of their data. If there had been discrimination resulting in blacks getting loans, even though they met the criteria, that would have meant they had been subjected to stricter criteria and therefore that their default rates on approved loans should have been lower. The fact that their default rates were the same meant that the ordinary criteria used for mortgages worked just fine, and the study therefore provided no evidence of discrimination.

Yet, consider the following remarkable exchange:

> "[That] is a sophisticated point," says Munnell, questioned by Forbes. She agrees that discrimination against blacks should show up in lower, not equal, default rates–discrimination would mean that good black applicants are being unfairly rejected. "You need that as a confirming piece of evidence. And we don't have it."
>
> Forbes: Did you ever ask the question that if defaults appear to be more or less the same among blacks and whites, that points to mortgage lenders making rational decisions?

> Munnell: No.
> Munnell does not want to repudiate her study. She tells Forbes, on reflection, that the census data are not good enough and could be "massaged" further: "I do believe that discrimination occurs."
> Forbes: You have no evidence?
> Munnell: I do not have evidence. ... No one has evidence.

To begin with, it must be noted that Brimelow and Spencer's point was not sophisticated at all. There was nothing arcane about it; on the contrary, there could have been nothing more basic. That it had not been anticipated in the study reveals something about the loss of critical functioning in the study's design and analysis. But what is more important is Munnell's statement "I do believe that discrimination occurs." For what could that belief have been based on? The study, corrected for the impact of default rates, did not support the conclusion. She admits this, but believes it anyway.

This belief, evidently, existed antecedent to the study and was independent of it, as we can see from the fact that the undermining of the empirical conclusion was not taken to bear upon it.

This was no small matter. Subsequent to the publication of the study, moves were taken to transform the credit approval criteria to increase the number of minority loans that would be approved. This was most notably accomplished through a mandated relaxation of standards imposed by the Department of Housing and Urban Development on Fannie Mae and Freddie Mac, the "Government Sponsored Entities" that bought mortgages from the original lenders (Schweitzer 2009), thereby absolving them of the risk.

The point to be made here is that the proponents and the critics of the view that discrimination was at work were living in two separate, incommensurable worlds. Between these worlds, some facts could be agreed, but the interpretations of these facts were entirely different.

I would like to suggest that they were apprehended through different frameworks of meaning or worldviews. In the absence of an agreed framework of meaning, it was inevitable that one worldview, in this case the view that discrimination was at work, would dominate the other by the mobilization of political power.

The argument I want to put forward is that the outcome of the political clash between these two worldviews was determined by a great deal of psychological weight. The view that the cause of inequality was discrimination was a moralistic view, which brought the other view under moral attack. The alternative view, based on a rational calculation of consequences, could not overcome such an attack because its own premise was undermined. It could not offer defense, but only reason. Yet reason itself had come under attack and was not able to defend itself. This points to a difficulty in our society far deeper and more threatening than the financial crisis itself.

The two frameworks of meaning are, of course, features of the two psychologies I have discussed: the Oedipal and the anti-Oedipal.

In what follows, I will lay out the differences between these two frameworks of meaning as it applies in this case. I will try to explain how reason itself comes under attack, and why it cannot defend itself against its moralistic opponent.

The Oedipal Framework

As we know, the core of meaning in Oedipal psychology is "objective self-consciousness," not in the sense of seeing oneself as one actually is, but as an object; that is to say from the perspective of someone who does not have a special emotional connection with us. It is developed through history, and is constantly under revision.

The objective framework, may be said to exist at a number of levels of abstraction. At the highest level, we have reason, logic, and mathematics, which we may think of as the structure of objectivity. These make possible the development of lower levels of abstraction, including the various laws and norms of society, structures of exchange, and understandings of objective reality that can be collectively comprehended, learned, negotiated, applied, and revised.

Specifically from the standpoint of social relations, the objective framework is what makes it possible to codify and comprehend the network of exchange relationships that form the structure of society. These are a set of widely accepted interlinked hypothetical propositions, most basically what Gouldner (1960) called the *norm of reciprocity*, of the form "If A does X, B will do Y." In such propositions, we can place ourselves either in the A position or the B position. This has made it possible for people to be mutually predictable and comprehensible to one another and to coordinate with each other.

Members of the society understand that other members will use this framework in the design of their own behavior, and hence they are dependent on this regularity. This understanding creates a generalized responsibility to act in accordance with these expectations, whether as norms that hold true for all members of the society, or as roles, which hold true for persons having specific functions. In this way, objectively established regularities are reinforced by moral and ethical motivations, but they are not any less objective for that.

The objective framework is not developed for its own sake. It serves subjective purposes. In the Freudian presentation, there is an implicit promise that if one becomes like father, one can have someone like mother. In other words, if you do what you're supposed to do in the objective world, you can attain your own desideratum, in the form of being again the center of a loving world, as you were when you were an infant, in the way that, as an adult, you imagine that coming about. Do what you are supposed to do, in one way of putting it, and you can be successful. Freud refers to this condition as the ego ideal. Hence, the objective framework gives us what we need to accomplish things collectively and cooperatively, while at the same time we each pursue the ego ideal, as we define it.

Now, the ego ideal is never fully realized; the world is not our mother, but objective self-consciousness make it possible to reconsider our behavior and the structure of exchange within which it occurs, and to reconfigure these to better attain the object of our desire. This leads to progress in the way we live our lives. It also makes it possible for us to account for, and to take responsibility for, the fact that we have not attained the ego ideal. It makes it possible for us to accept limitation and imperfection and to cope with frustration, to understand why we cannot have what we want just because we want it. These are perhaps no less important in determining the way we experience life, as we shall see.

But notice that while something is surely gained in objective self-consciousness, something is also lost. What is lost to objectivity is primary narcissism—the sense of one's cosmic importance, of being the center, and the meaning of the world just because one is who one is.

It stands to the favor of psychoanalytic theory that it can comprehend that what is lost is never really lost. Primary narcissism remains within every one of us and from that perspective the rage against the father, and hence against the social rules and common understandings that he represents, remain as well.

As we know, this makes possible another form of meaning, which is in a sense the opposite of Oedipal meaning, and consists in the rejection of the father and his intrusion into our fusion with mother.

Within this form, the power of father is illegitimate. He has taken mother by force and the rules and understandings through which he justifies his place are only a subterfuge to conceal and further his domination. There is no objectivity, but only the imposition of his subjective will and desire.

It is a lie, in other words, that we are not unique unto ourselves, occupying a special and central place in the universe. Reason, operating as it does through shared understanding that gives no special place to anyone's particular experience, cannot serve to limit our sense of importance, since it is itself based upon that very premise. We do not need to subordinate ourselves to this lie of our insignificance; all we need to do is to get rid of the liar. Expel him and his works and the connection with mother can be restored. Then the infinite power of her love and goodness will make life perfect for us.

Here again a world is structured, but the structure is the mirror image of Oedipal meaning. Expel the father, rather than identify with him; undermine his claims to legitimacy, rather than make sense of them. Do this and the perfect world of mother's love will be restored.

As we know, this is the basis of "political correctness."

Political correctness operates on the premise that there is no objective reality and hence that the achievements of the father in making reality amenable have been merely the means through which he has stolen mother's love. The structure of this world is determined by the presumption that he has stolen love more from some than from others. The bases of social action in this world are based on identification with those who have been especially victimized, and who are therefore able to make the strongest claim on all of our behalf. The father should be hated for his theft and the oppressed, which is to say those from whom he has most egregiously stolen love, should be loved in compensation.

What we can see here is a difference of ontology. The structure of the world is fundamentally different in the anti-Oedipal worldview than in the Oedipal. The Oedipal world is indifferent to us as individuals, and structured by objective social rules that apply to all of us. These rules are impersonal and we can hold them provisionally, but we rely on them and we know others will do so as well. This enables us to predict each other's behavior and creates our idea of rationality, based on this shared view of the world. Moreover, we depend on their doing so. A person's goodness or badness is determined by their behavior; it is a function of how they measure up to these rules and accept their responsibility to do so.

In the anti-Oedipal world the basic structural element is the conflict between the *I* and the *not-I* (Mead 1934). For the individual, the I is not only good, but is also the basis of all determinations of goodness. Therefore, the not-I is bad. Hence, the basic structural elements are not objective, impersonal rules, but moral conflicts in which good forces contend with bad forces. These designations of badness and goodness are absolute and cannot be changed by behavior. Good persons can do bad things, but this is because they have been forced to do so by bad forces, and they are therefore exculpated; their goodness has not been called into question.

And these bad forces include those objective, impersonal rules. As we have seen, their premise is that we see ourselves in a way that would apply to anyone; that we can locate ourselves indifferently as either A or B in the counterfactual expression *If A does X, B will do Y*. But the premise of the anti-Oedipal view is that our self is unique, and *sui generis*. Nothing else is like it. Thus, what are called objective rules are seen as part of the not-self. They imply the subjugation of the self, in its uniqueness; they represent a kind of death. It is therefore in the name of life that they are to be destroyed.

In the Oedipal worldview, the father is idealized, but this idealization is part of our image of the past. What marks the present are the rules of exchange that define social order and that count as his legacy. Justification is defined in terms of what a person does in accordance with these impersonal rules. In the anti-Oedipal worldview, the father is demonized, along with the rules of exchange, and even the rules of reason. In the Oedipal view, these rules are seen as his most important product, but in the anti-Oedipal view, they are seen as instruments of oppression. In this latter worldview, those who are defined through their antagonism to the father are idealized. Justification is defined in terms of their own spontaneity. It is celebrated if it is different from the rule bound behavior of the father, and particularly if it is opposed to it. Antagonism toward the father and his rules is the highest expression of the good person's identity.

It is very obvious that all of this will result in a very different interpretation of the meaning of credit worthiness.

The Meaning of Credit Worthiness in the Oedipal and Anti-Oedipal Worldviews

In the Oedipal worldview, credit worthiness is not a moral designation, but an economic calculation that represents the risk undertaken by someone making a loan. To be sure, whether someone fulfills their obligations may be used to evaluate them morally, but in this case it does not enter into the equation in a moral way. If there were a moral determination at issue, other morally relevant facts would be brought into consideration, such as what the person spent his or her money on. But no such facts are included. Instead, what is included is that, given certain empirically determinable circumstances, a certain percentage of people will not repay their loans. And this is entered into the equation, without moral commentary, as another objective fact.

By contrast, in the anti-Oedipal worldview, credit worthiness is an entirely moral concept. If someone is a member of a group that is understood as having been victimized by the father, that person is morally entitled to restitution. This often goes by the name of "social justice." As we saw, in the Oedipal worldview, moral considerations enter in a non-moral way. By contrast, within the anti-Oedipal worldview, economic factors enter in, but in a non-objective way. When data can be used to support the moral case, they are mobilized and employed; when they cannot, they are ignored or distorted until they do. That is the reason the economic calculations brought forward in the Boston Fed study could be so easily corrupted and abused, and why there was so little critical scrutiny applied to them. If the data could be used to support the charge of discrimination, they would be important in establishing the moral case; if not, they were, at best, of no interest.

This is a distinction that has the most profound consequences. We will return to it presently. First, the argument that supports it needs to be elaborated.

Closing the Gap

The claim that the anti-Oedipal worldview was responsible for the abuse of the research process in the Boston Fed study calls for further demonstration. For that purpose, I will turn to a guidebook called "Closing the GAP: A Guide to Equal Opportunity Lending," produced by the Federal Reserve Bank of Boston (1993) in the aftermath of the 1992 study, and intended to enunciate the conclusions to be drawn from it. According to Leibowitz (2008), it was clearly intended to be taken as speaking for the Federal Reserve System.

Closing the Gap manifests the tension between the Oedipal and anti-Oedipal views, but ultimately the former is subordinated to the latter. A look at the way the Fed's position was structured in this publication reveals much about the way this view of the world played out in their program recommendations. Two considerations are particularly significant.

In the first place, in accordance with the morality play ontology that structures the anti-Oedipal worldview, it denies the independent validity of objective economic considerations, and indeed redefines them as oppressive elements, essentially as racist. Second, it idealizes the minority groups in whose interest, supposedly, the loosening of credit standards is going to be accomplished. What it is essentially doing, therefore, is redefining the concept of credit worthiness in moral terms; taking the previous refusal of credit as a moral assault, which the loans are intended to rectify.

The Undermining of Objectivity

The subordination is actually rather explicit, and is evoked in a number of ways. For one thing, Closing the Gap provides sidebars which lay out the thrust of their position by citing authorities. For example, they quote Lawrence B. Lindsey, identified as "Member, Board of Governors of the Federal Reserve System" as saying "The regulatory issues in the 1990s will not be limited to safety and soundness, but will increasingly emphasize fairness: whether or not banks are fulfilling the needs of their communities." Notice here that the universality of application is not seen as "fulfilling the needs of their communities," which the Oedipal worldview would expect. Rather, this is set in opposition to something called "fairness," which must mean that those "communities" represent specific groups whose interests have been subordinated in the past and which now, in the interest of goodness, should be furthered. Who these specific communities are is defined in another sidebar:

> Editors 'Note: A 1992 study of mortgage lending by the Federal Reserve Bank of Boston analyzed the effects of race on denial rates for blacks and Hispanics in the Boston metropolitan area. However, around the country, members of other racial and ethnic groups may also experience credit dis-

crimination. For editorial purposes, it was necessary to select a single term to refer to underserved borrowers. In this publication, the terms "minority" or "minority group" are used to refer to borrowers, including blacks and Hispanics, who are not members of the dominant culture in a particular lending area.

And it is clear that there is muscle behind this program. Here is another sidebar:

Did You Know? Failure to comply with the Equal Credit Opportunity Act or Regulation B can subject a financial institution to civil liability for actual and punitive damages in individual or class actions. Liability for punitive damages can be as much as $10,000 in individual actions and the lesser of $500,000 or 1 percent of the creditor's net worth in class actions

The seriousness of these penalties must be taken into consideration in order to understand the subordination of objectivity to this moral program, which is accomplished in other, more indirect ways. Most importantly, the meaning of the term "discrimination" becomes indeterminate and impossible to pin down, but loses none of the opprobrium or the threat attached to it.

Thus, the authors acknowledge that "discrimination" may be of three types:

For the purposes of this publication, we distinguish among three types of discrimination: overt, intentional discrimination; subtle, deliberate discrimination; and unintentional discrimination.

They acknowledge that "Overt discrimination in mortgage lending is rarely seen today."

Discrimination is more likely to be subtle, reflected in the failure to market loan products to potential minority customers and the failure of lenders to hire and promote staff from racial and ethnic minority groups.

Students of organizations will understand that, the penalties for "discrimination" being as serious as they are, a bit of preemptive selective hiring and promotion will be useful as a defense, and will therefore be prudent, whether or not it serves a rational business purpose. Notice, however, that this has not been said. A policy has been moved along here by innuendo, not through conscious reason, and in this regard may again be said to be an undermining of objectivity.

But for present purposes, what is most interesting is the third form of "discrimination":

> Unintentional discrimination may be observed when a lender's underwriting policies contain arbitrary or outdated criteria that effectively disqualify many urban or lower–income minority applicants.

What can "arbitrary" and "outdated" mean here? The term arbitrary could mean simply that there is no reason for the criteria, but any bank would not need to be told this. Rather, it would seem to mean that the rules are arbitrary in the sense that they are expressions of one culture, but not of others. What is missing here is a sense of the instrumental character of the rules; their purpose in enabling people to gain their objectives through following rules that make sense for that purpose, as rules within the Oedipal worldview are intended to do.

The idea that these rules are the product of objective observation and rational utilitarian calculation is no longer present. Within the anti-Oedipal worldview, those considerations are not recognized. But deprived of that rationale, such rules can only be seen as one way of doing things, of no distinctive merit, rather than another. That is the sense in which they are seen as arbitrary here.

In the absence of any more substantive critique, the other term of opprobrium, "outdated criteria," can only mean those criteria that the times, moved by whatever political and moralizing currents prevail, now call for abandoning. Here again, what is missing is the idea that the rules have a purpose that is better furthered by one set of rules than another, and that changes in rules are the result of rational considerations determining which rules are more likely to attain that purpose.

What we can see here is that within the anti-Oedipal worldview, the gap between the person and the ego ideal has been rendered anomalous. There is and can be no good reason why one simply cannot do as one wants and be loved for it. The idea that one must become like father has revealed itself as paternal propaganda. Instead of being the route to the ego ideal, the paternal legacy of rules is seen as what is blocking the enjoyment of maternal embrace. They are not to be followed, but destroyed.

Reason counts for nothing in these matters, and standing on the ground of reason can only lead to trouble. And this is in a matter where getting a judgment wrong can mean heavy fines and opprobrium. The next paragraph spells out what must follow from this:

> While the banking industry is not expected to cure the nation's social and racial ills, lenders do have a specific legal responsibility to ensure that negative perceptions, attitudes, and prejudices do not systematically affect the fair and even-handed distribution of credit in our society. Fair lending must be an integral part of a financial institution's business plan.

Thus, insofar as lending is based on rational criteria, those criteria are redefined, when they stand in the way of political and moral currents, as "negative perceptions, attitudes, and prejudices." Indeed, it does not go too far to say that skepticism about the unlikelihood of a person with a poor history of loan repayment paying their loan would be classified as prejudice under these designations.

This has much to do with the way political correctness was able to carry the day in the issue of relaxing lending criteria. It set rational justification of the rules, based on objective considerations, as deeply immoral and, potentially, dangerously illegal. Discrimination could have been anything. It had nothing to do with intent, and could have represented criteria that had, for reasons that could not have been foreseen or predicted, come to be seen as "outdated" or "arbitrary". But it was no less punishable for that. Few could have been expected to stand in the face of such potential criticism, and these low expectations were not, in the event, exceeded.

One is reminded here of Orwell's observation that a Party member must not only have the correct thoughts, but also the correct instincts. One can think of no better index of the undermining of the rational comprehension of objective reality—the paternal function—than this.

Idealization of the Oppressed

The anti-Oedipal worldview is structured by the tension between the forces of badness, represented by the father whose rules are arbitrary and self-serving, and the oppressed, who represent the forces of goodness. The maternal forces operate here as oppressed, to be sure, but also in love and fusion with the oppressed.

In the Oedipal worldview, the father was conceived to have the mother's love, and that is the sense in which he was idealized. In the anti-Oedipal view, it is the oppressed who have mother's love, and hence it is they who are idealized.

The anti-Oedipal worldview preserves and defends the individual's uniqueness and spontaneity. Idealization takes the form of the belief that whatever the idealized one naturally and spontaneously does is lovable. Mother's love attaches to him because he is who he is. The proper response to him, therefore, is to see him in the best possible light. Negative behavior can be acknowledged here, but it must be attributed to forces outside of his control: his environment, discrimination, and so on. Anything but unconditional love, including judgments made on the basis of universalistic criteria, is seen as bad: bigotry, prejudice, and the like.

Idealization of the oppressed implies demonization of anything that would deny their absolute uniqueness and impinge on their spontaneity. All rules do that; they are therefore anathema and should be undermined. This can be seen in the form of the treatment of exceptions to the rules of credit worthiness.

These are of critical importance because of the fact that the crisis was caused by people being unable to pay the mortgages they were awarded under the loosened criteria, which took the form of authorizing and mandating exceptions to the rules that would otherwise have been applied. The exceptions, that is to say, were a cause of the crisis.

In evaluating their use, we have the benefit of hindsight. We are not looking at them to ascertain their validity; they were not valid. Rather, what is important is to understand how that invalidity entered into the system.

The main point is that these exceptions were not treated as exceptions, but as the bases of policy in their own right. For example:

> Even the most determined lending institution will have difficulty cultivating business from minority customers if its underwriting standards contain arbitrary or unreasonable measures of creditworthiness.
>
> Consistency in evaluating loan applications is also critical to ensuring fair treatment. Since many mortgage applicants who are approved do not meet every underwriting guideline, lending policies should have mechanisms that define and monitor the use of compensating factors to ensure that they are applied consistently, without regard to race or ethnicity.

But the matter of consistency must be seen as a term of art, since the exceptions became a major factor in evaluating loan applications only when the move was made to maximize lending to minorities. Consistency can only mean that if an exception has been made for anybody, on a certain basis, that basis should be available to everybody. In this way, the exception became the rule.

Again, they say:

> Special care should be taken to ensure that standards are appropriate to the economic culture of urban, lower–income, and nontraditional consumers.

This refers back to the idea that the choice of cultures, and hence of the rules they follow, is arbitrary. This again says something about exceptions, in the form of difference from instrumental norms, determining the thrust of policy.

Moreover, such policies should be made known to minority mortgage applicants.

> To ensure fair treatment, it is important that the lending institution document its policies and practices regarding acceptable compensating factors. If an institution permits flexibility in applying underwriting standards, it must do so consistently. Management should consider developing a checklist for loan production staff to ensure that all allowable compensating factors are requested of the borrower (such as explanations of late debt payments or a demonstrated ability to carry high housing costs). The checklist will also make loan production staff aware of the institution's commitment to serving borrowers who may not meet traditional underwriting standards.
>
> Informed borrowers are more likely to ask loan production staff about ways to enhance their applications. Thus, another way to encourage consistent treatment is by clearly communicating the institution's lending policies and underwriting standards to the public.

Looking at the substance of these exceptions, the idea that they have been transformed into policy is again manifest. And their exploration leads us to a further understanding of what lies behind the Fed's approach. Consider this:

> In reviewing past credit problems, lenders should be willing to consider extenuating circumstances. For lower–income applicants in particular, unforeseen expenses can have a disproportionate effect on an otherwise positive credit record. In these instances, paying off past bad debts or establishing a regular repayment schedule with creditors may demonstrate a willingness and ability to resolve debts.

What we see here are two things. First, consistent with what we saw before, looking for reasons to apply exceptions has become the policy. Second, part of the application of that program has become a mandated optimism about the willingness and ability of the applicant to repay the loan. Thus, simply establishing a payment schedule is supposed, by itself, to demonstrate such willingness and ability. Similarly:

> Successful participation in credit counseling or buyer education programs is another way that applicants can demonstrate an ability to manage their debts responsibly.

Leibowitz (2008) is scathing about the way these exceptions systematically violated rational considerations:

> Traditional lending standards were attacked as a form of discrimination by regulators and housing advocates. It was claimed that mortgage applicants could handle larger obligation ratios than those imposed by traditional standards; that mortgage applicants could make their monthly payments without having been consistently at a job; that mortgage applicants didn't need to be able to show that they could come up with a down payment—a gift, say from a phony charity set up by the seller of the home, would do just fine. It was suggested that mortgage applicants should be deemed credit-worthy if the applicants watched some sort of educational video about the housing market and the mortgage process. This was all nonsense, one lie compounding another.
>
> The claim that lending standards could be "relaxed" without increasing the number of defaults was false. When you build a housing market on such false claims, you are asking for trouble.

But Leibowitz' point here is the assignment of blame, and that is not my purpose. The point here is to get at the psychodynamics underlying these disastrous moves. For that purpose, the proper focus is again the shift from the Oedipal to the anti-Oedipal worldview as represented in a shift in the meaning of making a loan.

Summary

In the Oedipal view, the function of the lending institution is to connect lender and borrower in a way that benefits both of them. The rules of credit worthiness function to ensure that mutuality of benefit, based on the premise that the borrower and the lender will operate within an objective framework of shared normative and legal understanding.

Thus, in the Oedipal worldview, based on objective rules of exchange, the idea that a loan is to be repaid is part of the definition of a loan; in the anti-Oedipal worldview, it is not.

In the anti-Oedipal worldview, a loan is an expression of love, existing by itself and without regard to consequences. In the final analysis, the function of the lending institution is to express love of the oppressed by giving them money. The rules of mutual understanding are not seen as a framework that ensures mutual benefit and minimizes risk, but as obstacles, and every care is undertaken to find ways around them. Characteristics of the lender that have been established to minimize risk are seen as violations of culture and the imposition of alien understandings. They are replaced by an idealization, which effectively assumes that borrowers should be seen in the most favorable light. The loan is to be made, not if certain qualifications are passed, but if circumstances can be imagined in which the application of the qualifications may be considered not fair. Indeed, skepticism about this reversal may be seen as representing a bigoted attitude that itself constitutes discrimination.

But the result we have seen follows from the premise. The anti-Oedipal worldview is based on the assumption that objective reality does not exist and that the rules developed to take it into account are impositions and agencies of aggression. Yet there is an external world and violation of the prudential rules that keep us safe cannot be without consequences, for the borrower as much as for the lender.

Conclusion: The Legacy of the Father

I have been operating on the assumption that the loosening of credit standards on the grounds of political correctness was one of the causes of the sub-prime crisis, but not necessarily the only one. I do not know what weight to give to the considerations adduced here. I suspect that the weight is substantial, but I need to introduce the caveat that the range of its applicability is uncertain.

The objective view of social reality, the legacy of the father, building on itself, and building on itself, again and again, has resulted, in a capacity to predict and plan that is by no means inconsiderable. This is best exemplified in the field of economics, but such a capacity is not unique to that discipline. Politicians, for example, by polling techniques, can gain a sense of where the public is at any given time, and as a result can craft their activities to better serve the people's desires. This has its advantages and its disadvantages, but the truth is also that the objective view of social reality enables us to assess those advantages and disadvantages, and build our considerations into the next iteration. The view of reality as indifferent holds little appeal for those who require a millennial outcome, but it does offer a sense of the narcissism involved in any such demand, and it gives us a profound understanding of the damage that narcissism can create.

The anti-Oedipal worldview is driven by narcissism, though this fact has been obscured by the absolutistic moralism within which it arises. This moralism is based on the idea that it is an expression of mother's love, but this is true only to a very limited extent. The mother at issue is not a real mother, but a child's fantasy of the mother that has been lost; who was made out of love for the child and was the whole world. She is, functionally speaking, the complement to the child's primary narcissism.

But the child needs to abandon its primary narcissism because the world is not its mother. Acting as if it were will lead the child to catastrophe. And acting in the name of the world as mother is not compassionate, but feckless. By encouraging irresponsibility, it devastates those it would help.

This mother is a fantasy, but she is a fantasy that represents infinite benevolence and omnipotence. Identify with her and you incorporate this omnipotence and benevolence into yourself. Of course, this is fantasy as well, but one can understand that, from within this fantasy, the expulsion of the father, flawed and limited as he is, and the external reality that he represents, would feel right and moral. So in the end, such moralism takes the indifference of reality as unworthy, and calls for its destruction, in the name of goodness. But there is no real sense in which, in the real world in which, in fact, we all live, it was an act of goodness to lend money to people who could not repay those loans. They lost those homes, and also lost the hopes and dreams that went with them.

Of course they were not alone in their suffering. The chaos in the system that was due in part to the lowering of standards brought devastation to everyone else. It could have been predicted, but it was not predicted because the dynamic that launched it destroyed the possibility of prediction as well.

Taken to its extreme, narcissism is nihilistic, and aimed at the destruction of anything outside the self, and outside the loving mother who is its mirror. This must include everyone who is seen as another, which is to say everyone with whom we do not identify. Anyone who can see beyond himself will recognize that if each self takes everyone else as its enemy, the result can only be Hobbes's "state of nature." But of course it requires the paternal function, the objective view of social reality, to make that observation.

The anti-Oedipal framework does not recognize rules, but only exceptions to rules. In accordance with the premise that identifies the individual with his uniqueness, exceptions are supposed to replace rules as the organizing principle of society. But this would be an impossibility. Exceptions are exceptions to rules; there cannot be exceptions unless there are rules.

The anti-Oedipal framework offers itself as an alternative form of social organization, but it undermines itself. What it presses toward is not an alternative form of social organization, but chaos. This is a fact that, in our anti-Oedipal times, needs to be taken seriously. But taking it seriously would require an understanding of what, objectively, will lead to what.

Anyone so inclined can do the math on this. The alternative is to have faith that mother will provide.

References

Brimelow, Peter, and Leslie Spencer. 1993. The Hidden Clue. *Forbes*, January 4.

Day, Theodore E., and Stan J. Liebowitz. 1998. Mortgage Lending to Minorities: Where's The Bias? *Economic Inquiry* (January): 1–27.

Federal Reserve Bank of Boston. 1993. *Closing the GAP: A Guide to Equal Opportunity Lending*. Boston, MA: Federal Reserve Bank of Boston.

Gouldner, Alvin W. 1960. The Norm of Reciprocity: A Preliminary Statement. *American Sociological Review* 25: 161–178.

Liebowitz, Stan. 2008. Statement of Stan Liebowitz Before the House Subcommittee on the Constitution, Civil Rights, and Civil Liberties Hearing on Enforcement of the Fair Housing Act of 1968, June 12.

Mead, George Herbert. 1934. *Mind, Self, and Society*. ed. C.W. Morris. Chicago: University of Chicago Press.

Munnell, Alicia H., Lynn E. Browne, James McEneaney, and Geoffrey M.B. Tootell. 1996. Mortgage Lending in Boston: Interpreting HMDA Data. *American Economic Review* 86(1): 25–53.

Schweitzer, Peter. 2009. *Architects of Ruin*. New York: HarperCollins.

Sowell, Thomas. 2009. *The Housing Boom and Bust*. New York: Basic Books.

CHAPTER 6

Analysis of the British Riots of 2011

(with Andreas Liefooghe)

The fires of a burning England were not out before its most prestigious and prominent voices began delivering their verdict on what had caused them. The rioters were poor and the government had cut their support, taking away all that they had. Society had raised them to believe they needed to have certain consumer objects, but then it had not given them the means to obtain these things, so they had no way of getting them except through theft. The police were racist and treated people disrespectfully, intolerably so. Prominent figures in the government and the economy were corrupt; the rioters were no worse, and perhaps were even taking their cue from them. And so on.

But there was one thing about these judgments, expressing the views of what we will call the cultural elite, that all had in common, which was that it was society, specifically its central, defining institutions, that was at fault. The rioters were just doing what anyone would do in the circumstances they were in. It was society that created those circumstances and, therefore, it was society that was to blame for its own destruction.

There is a problem that arises from seeing things in this way. If society, through its cultural elite, accepts that it was responsible for the riots, then it effectively justifies them; it shifts the guilt from the rioters to society itself. The forces of innocence were attacking the forces of corruption and injustice. What side should a good person be on, anyway? But if society

H.S. Schwartz, *Political Correctness and the Destruction of Social Order*, DOI 10.1007/978-3-319-39805-1_6

is so unjust that rioting is people's only recourse, how can it see itself as worth maintaining?

The point is not that any social criticism poses a threat to society. On the contrary, a healthy society is not only not endangered by criticism, but it positively needs criticism to stay healthy. The matter here is one of balance; it is the unanimity of negative opinion here that indicates the problem. When Joseph Schumpeter spoke of "creative destruction," he did not mean that destruction, by itself, is creative. He meant that alongside the destructive processes were constructive ones that could thrive in the space created by the destruction. But creativity flourishes amidst positive feelings about the self, not self-hatred.

The result of that self-hatred may be that society does not feel morally entitled to rise in its own defense. Weakening society's capacity to defend itself would cause the forces seeking to destroy it to become relatively stronger, even to the extent of putting society in jeopardy. In that case, the balance of power within society would be altered. We would have an inversion of power. How did this inversion of power come about?

In this chapter, we will attempt to answer this question by putting forward an analysis of the role played by political correctness in preparing the grounds for the unfolding scenario.

Political Correctness

The condemnation of society that leads to holding it responsible for the riots, hence to the inversion of power, is, itself, a product of society. It did not develop after the riots, but is a cultural configuration that has been in operation for a long time. The riots, in a sense, simply provided it with a new occasion for its expression. We call this cultural configuration political correctness.

The connection between the riots and political correctness is quite close. Looked at from within our psychoanalytic point of view, they are kindred; two phenomena with different appearances, but the same meaning, which they are playing out in different registers. They can reinforce each other, lending strength to one another and even making the other possible.

We will inquire both in a general way and with specific regard to an important element of the riots: namely, the hesitation of the police to impose order, either by mobilizing sufficient police power in what was clearly a dangerous situation or through a reluctance on the part of the available police to impose order. This had terrible consequences, in that the rioters saw that they could get away with doing whatever they wanted, and led others to join the riots in a massive way.

All are agreed that, together with the assist provided by modern electronic communication, this resulted in a powerful acceleration of the riots. As it was put by an interviewee for the official Interim Report of the Riots Communities and Victims Panel, 2011 (henceforth RCVP):

> On the night of the riots in Tottenham, there were not enough police on the streets and the ones that were there failed to contain the riot. They stood back and watched as people set fire to everything and anything. … We were left to fend for ourselves. If the police had intervened earlier, I believe the scale of the riots could have been prevented and my home could have been saved. (RCVP, p. 43)

The theme of police abandonment was common. For example,

> Local people in Haringey were extremely upset and angry that the police did not intervene as the riots grew. Many felt they had been left to fend for themselves. Residents and businesses on the High Road felt they had been abandoned. (RCVP, p. 41)

And, generally:

> In the Panel's meetings with victims and communities there has been a significant theme of abandonment. For many the absence of police on the streets was deeply shocking. (RCVP, p. 106)

So:

> In our analysis the images of police being seen to "backoff" in Tottenham and their rapid circulation across social media and broadcast news services conveyed a loss of control of the streets. This combined with a febrile rumour environment created a unprecedented explosive cocktail. "The streets were there for the taking." (Ibid.)

The failure of the police to impose order made ordinary citizens fear for their own safety, property, and rights, thus increasing a sense of overwhelming insecurity at all levels of society. Our claim is that it was, in some significant measure, a product of political correctness.

Further on, we will look at the underlying dynamics of political correctness, but first we need to get some sense of the nature of riots.

Psychodynamics of Riots

The key to the psychoanalytic understanding of riots is that, at the most basic level, there is not very much that needs to be explained. At the roots, the psychodynamics of a riot are quite straightforward. What calls for understanding is the fact that people are not rioting all the time.

This was the essence of Freud's classic book *Civilization and its Discontents.* What he presented was the view that there is a "death instinct," an innate aggressiveness that drives toward destruction in human beings, indeed in all living things.

But the necessities of civilization require that we renounce this instinct in its pure form. Freud was famously ambivalent about this renunciation and mindful of the fragility of the institutions that it creates.

> [I]t is impossible to overlook the extent to which civilization is built up on a renunciation of instinct, how much it presupposes precisely the non-satisfaction (by suppression, repression or some other means?) of powerful instincts. This "cultural frustration" dominates the large field of social relationships between human beings. As we already know, it is the cause of the hostility against which all civilizations have to struggle. (Freud 1962, p. 44)

So civilization is based on the renunciation of instincts, but it wears this "cultural frustration" uneasily. Aggressiveness is a permanent force that is always just underneath the surface and capable of breaking out any time the renunciation lapses.

Now, this renunciation of instincts, Freud says, takes two forms: suppression and repression, depending on whether the cause is external or internal. In the case of suppression, we renounce our instinctual aggression under the threat of physical punishment at the hands of authority. In the case of repression, we internalize authority, originally the parents and specifically the father, to form the superego, which gives our aggression back to us in the form of guilt.

Political correctness is an attack upon the father (Schwartz 2003, 2010), who represents authority. As such, it undermines both of the ways in which instinctual renunciation takes place. This leaves the aggressive instinct, always just underneath the surface, to express itself without constraint. That is what we saw in the riots.

Oedipal and Anti-Oedipal Psychology

Our way of understanding political correctness arises from what we have called anti-Oedipal psychology, which is defined against Oedipal psychology.

As we know, anti-Oedipal psychology is Oedipal psychology turned upside down. The child's view of father is the opposite of what it is in Oedipal psychology. Father has not gained mother's love by his accomplishments; they cannot be worth anything. He must have gained his presence with her through the commission of fraud and violence. It was not due to a legitimate process that the child would have to accept, it was illegitimate; it was an act of theft.

Now, the child is not just seeing his own case here; in effect, this is the lens through which he sees the world. The father's theft of love from the child would be seen especially to apply to those groups, such as various minorities, that have not had love in the past. Mother's love has been stolen from them in a systematic way. That systematic theft is what the father does, and indeed what the father is. The society that he has created and runs is rotten and corrupt at its core. It is a structure of oppression and nothing but oppression. It deserves to be destroyed. Destroying it would bring about the return to mother's love. That would be a good and righteous act.

In the interim, the consequences of his acts should be registered. The father should be hated, and those who have been unloved in the past, the groups from whom he has stolen love, should be loved in compensation; indeed, they should be idealized. Their claims against the father and the society that represents his theft should be supported.

This gives us the basic dynamic of political correctness. We can see how it underlies some of the dynamics of the British riots. It does not explain everything; perhaps not even most of it. For example, the Interim Report lists a number of distinct types of rioters with, no doubt, quite different motivations, including organized crime types who surely thought of this as just a good day's work.

But if one may speak of a meaning of the riots within the context of our own time—and this would certainly include those attempts to justify them that we saw coming from the cultural elite—anti-Oedipal psychology offers a useful perspective. Whatever else the riots were, they were certainly an attack upon the father and his works.

Before looking further into this, there are a few points that it would be useful to make, largely concerning the nature of the father's works. As we have seen, among the most important works of the father has been to create and maintain social order. This was the accomplishment that made the other accomplishments possible.

We need to recall how fragile social order is. For Freud, it rests on a renunciation of the instincts, most notably of aggression. In Freud's account, this renunciation rests either upon the fear of brute force, or on the internalization of an idealized father to form the superego. Then, aggression is turned inward in the form of guilt. But take away the idealization of the father and brute force is all that remains. This force may not be present directly, but when the idealization of the father is lost, what is lost along with it is the *sense* of the renunciation, the idea that it has a purpose and is something one ought to do. When that happens, aggression is no longer bound by the conscience and turned inward, but available to be turned outward at any provocation, or even any opportunity in which external punishment can be avoided. Indeed, vestiges of the conscience can even be understood as internalized oppression.

Also important is that the father is in the boundary business. It was not the father that caused the separation of infant and child, but reality itself. The father is the personification of reality as it is first experienced. But he can choose to actively engage what he previously suffered passively. This defines his role, which is to build on this connection. Dealing with reality, and creating a boundary between harsh external reality and the family, where mother's love can then flow freely and safely, becomes his special contribution (Schwartz 2003).

To deny the value of the father's works means denying the need for a boundary. Mother's love should become the organizing principle of the world. With it, we would be able to operate safely without boundaries, limits, or constraint. There could be no such things as real enemies, only other children who have not been sufficiently loved. We would all be able to do what we want, to act on our impulses with impunity and in perfect safety.

This would have the effect of redefining the concept of the self. In Oedipal psychology, the self is imagined to be separate from the world, which is for the most part indifferent to it. In anti-Oedipal psychology, separation is no longer considered normal; the very idea of indifference disappears and the self is imagined to live in a world that revolves around it with love: an image that we have called "the pristine self."

Anything other than love would be experienced as a violation of the self. Most importantly for our purposes, that would apply to indifference, which would be redefined as hate, and which would include the indifferent application of the law.

This would be particularly so for those defined as oppressed, which is to say those who have been deprived in the past. They should be able to do what they want, without regard to the law, and with a sense of enhanced entitlement, seeing it, indeed, as the manifestation of justice and morality. The rioters could see themselves in this way and the politically correct, whose idea it was in the first place, would agree.

In the next section, we will show how a number of these concepts played out in the riots, largely using material from interviews with the rioters, which can be helpful in conveying their states of mind.

Anti-Oedipal Psychology and the Riots

As we have said, the purpose of the father's work was to bring him closer to the ego ideal; at the social level, that means gaining society's love in the form of social standing. In our society, undoubtedly, the primary symbol of the ego ideal is wealth. Wealth, then, is the symbol of attainment of the ego ideal. If the value of the father's works is denied, there is no way of justifying why some should have the symbols of the ego ideal, of social standing, while others do not. Rather, within the concept of the pristine self, one is entitled to the ego ideal just because one is who one is. In the words of one, which caught the attention of many, "We're worth it."

This idea of the riots as resulting from rage arising from a violated sense of entitlement is common in the conceptions of the rioters, and helps them explain themselves to themselves in ways that others just don't get.

Andrew, a 16-year-old student, says:

> Police don't think we're rioting for a reason. They believe we're rioting because Mark Duggan died and we have no other reason. Like, we're rioting 'cos they're not giving us nothing to do, they're taking away EMA [educational maintenance allowance], taking away free travel, taking away certain allowances that teenagers have and they're not replacing it with anything good. (Lewis 2011)

Similarly, if others have it, while you do not, they must have stolen it from you. Property, in the anarchist Proudhon's terms, comes to be seen as theft. The wealth of others, that is to say, is a symbol of injustice and a suitable target of righteous destruction.

Charley, another student, was caught up in running battles with the police. He said:

> There must have been at least 200 people … It was just a horde, like a mosh pit … Cars got destroyed. Boss cars. Like Beemer, Mercedes. I'm sitting there watching kids just rain stones on them. (ibid.)

And taking the symbols of wealth and social standing for yourself simply returns things to their proper order.

Omar, a poor 16-year old from the suburbs, had taken the train into Birmingham city centre. New clothes were a special treat for him, but not just for the sake of the clothes themselves. In the torn and dirty clothing he usually wore, he felt that "people with money, good families," looked down on him:

> I hate feeling like people are judging me. They don't know about me and then they just look at you and I hate it, I absolutely hate it.

But, regarding his new looted track suit:

> [W]hen I get new clothes I feel better … They will have to look down at someone else. (ibid.)

So one can easily understand that the riots, which unleashed vast amounts of destructive energy against the very structure of society, could have appeared to the rioters, not only as legitimate, but as righteous. This typically took the form of a celebration of attacks upon the law and the police, who were widely seen as illegitimate: "The police are the biggest gang out there."

Some interviews make clear the connection between the police role and suppression of the instincts, and the ease with which aggression is unleashed when that suppression stops.

This is from James, a 19-year-old student who originally joined the riots to fight the police, with no intention of stealing anything, but stayed to take what he could:

> Someone came up with the idea: if we spread this, could the police like control it? … I think the looting came about because it was linked to police … We're showing them that, yeah, we're bigger than the police, we are actually bigger than the police. Fair enough, we are breaking the law and everything, but there's more of us than there are of you. So if we want to do this, we can do this. And you won't do anything to stop us. (ibid.)

Antagonism toward the police can be seen in almost all of the interviews with the rioters. For example, Alex, a 32-year-old white rioter from South London, recounts how he stepped out of a pub in Tottenham to find the early stages of the riot. An abandoned police car had been set on fire, and young people were throwing bottles at the police. He watched as they pushed another police car into a wall, where it rolled back into the street. He saw them smash the windows and place a black garbage bag on the seat. Then he joined the action:

> It was the police car—I know what they stand for … For the record: yeah, I do hate the fucking police … I was caught up in the situation. And it was like: let's cause fucking chaos—let's cause a riot … I went up, put my head in there—the front-seat window—set light to the black bag and walked away from there and just slowly watched it, and everybody was cheering. (ibid.)

Then he watched as the gas tank blew up. The images of the two burning police cars flashed through thousands of mobile phones, enticing a myriad of others to join the mêlée.

And, from another rioter:

> I thought, wow, like, there's actually a force against the government, and I thought of it as like a battle, like a war, that was starting like, to put it into perspective. To put the riots into perspective, I thought of it as a war between the youth and the government, police. I think the youth and people in general and the government is opposing … so that's why I think of it as a war. The world right now is unjust. Society, how I feel, it's unjust. When I went outside for the first time, I could feel like, that the air was, it wasn't how it normally was, it was like an unspoken kind of feeling just floating around. It actually made me feel really strong. It made me feel really powerful. (Carter 2011)

An important aspect of this was the rioters' justification of their behavior by reference to the supposedly abusive behavior of the police. This particular justification was wholeheartedly embraced by the cultural elite. The report "Reading the Riots," a joint project of the *Guardian* newspaper and the London School of Economics (Rusbridger and Rees 2011), took it entirely at face value and placed this claim at the very center of their analysis. They said that 85 % of the rioters they interviewed said that policing was an "important" or "very important" factor in the riots (p. 20).

The focal point for this tension with the police was a tactic called "stop and search," where police search persons that they pick up on the streets whom they have reason to believe have committed a crime. Most of the rioters had been subjected to this tactic, which had been disproportionately applied to black people, in terms of their fraction of the population, and blamed the riots on the aggressive and discourteous manner with which it was employed.

Of course, it is possible that the British police, supposedly marinated in racism, had been so abusive in their treatment of black people that a revolt, in the form of the riots, was understandable. But our analysis, as it points to the inherent antagonism in anti-Oedipal psychology, between the pristine self and objective social order, suggests another possibility.

According to the official Interim Report (Riots Communities and Victims Panel 2011) those arrested for rioting had committed, on average, 11 previous offences and of those who had committed prior offences, the average number was 14. Eighty-eight percent of those arrested had been previously "known to the police" as a result of having been previously arrested, convicted, or cautioned (p. 29). As senior officials were reported in the Final Report (Riots Communities and Victims Panel 2012) to have said: "[A]s 9 out of 10 arrested rioters were known to the police, it is not surprising that they cited poor relationships as a motivational factor" (p. 24).

With specific regard to the tactic of stop and search, pulling someone off the street and searching them is by nature aggressive and disturbing. Being treated on the premise that one may be a criminal is a violation of one's dignity and is going to be felt that way by anyone who does not credit the reasonableness of the police action. But the capacity for seeing the reasonableness of police action arises from seeing one's behavior from the standpoint of society's common framework of objective self-understanding. Yet that comes from the internalization of the father, which is, according to the present theory, exactly what was being rejected here.

Rather, the evident feeling of grievance suggests a level of entitlement characteristic of the pristine self. Such a person would see police as being abusive even when they were doing their job in an entirely proper fashion.

The chapter up until now offers an explanation for the outset of the riots. The continuation of the riots needs further explanation, since the agencies of social control could have contained this aggression directed against society by doing their traditional work of countering that aggression by harsh punishment. Yet this did not happen. We need to ask why not.

What Happened to the Forces of Social Order?

There is agreement among observers and the public that the police hesitated to impose order and that this hesitation was widely noted and served as an accelerant to the riots, transforming them from local occurrences to a large-scale frenzy.

In effect, this absence of police had a profound impact not only on the course of the riots as such but also on a sense of public disbelief and growing social anxiety that law and order were not being maintained as expected.

To understand this hesitation, we need to see what impact anti-Oedipal psychology and political correctness had upon the police, who were, after all, the agents of the now rejected superego.

The view we will offer here is that the police were required, even within the context of their normal functioning, to turn their aggression against themselves and see themselves as an oppressive force. The rioters, in other words, were justified in directing their aggression outward, but police were required to turn their aggression inward; they were the ones who were supposed to feel guilty. We can think of the result as the castration of the British police. In order to understand how this came about, we need to engage with the issue of race, and with the history of the police's relationship to that issue.

The Castration of the British Police Through Political Correctness

At the outset, the rioters were overwhelmingly black. Later on, they became quite multi-ethnic, but if one is looking to understand the initial hesitancy, the orientation of the police toward the black community suggests itself as a good place to start the analysis.

Within the framework of political correctness, black people have been designated as the paradigmatic oppressed group, from whom love has been stolen by the father. Now, within the logic of political correctness, objective social structures are not recognized as objective, but are seen as agencies of oppression. The result is that, for many black people, objective social structures have come to be seen as agencies for the specific oppression of black people, which is to say racist.

The dictates of political correctness require that, in pursuance of the demand for love of the oppressed, this interpretation be validated. The effect has been to categorize police practice as racist, even if the police are doing exactly what they are supposed to do to in order to maintain law and order.

The Case of Stephen Lawrence

To show how this developed in Britain, a look at history is necessary. Specifically, one must consider the aftermath of the murder on the night of 22 April 1993 of a young black man named Stephen Lawrence.

Lawrence, a person whose blamelessness in this incident has never been seriously questioned was, along with a friend named Duwayne Brooks, waiting for a bus in a predominately white area of South London. He was set upon by a group of five or six young white thugs. One of the thugs shouted "What, what! Nigger!" and stabbed Lawrence who died of his wounds.

The police investigation of the murder, which involved up to 25 police officers, was soon focused, based on information from people in the neighborhood, on a group known as the Acourt gang. We now know, on the basis of DNA analysis, that these were, indeed, the attackers. However, at that time, although several members of the gang were arrested, the evidence was ruled by the Crown Prosecution Service to be inadequate to sustain a conviction, and they had to be released.

But by this time the incident had become an international cause célèbre, and this dénouement was unacceptable. So the investigation continued and was reinvigorated. It was lavishly resourced, and included the placement of videotape equipment in the apartment of one of the members of the gang, where they frequently gathered. Still, the authorities did not acquire information which they believed would be sufficient evidence for a conviction.

The Lawrence family, however, could not accept this judgment and began a private prosecution of some of the gang members, which commenced on 17 April 1996. In that trial, which received full police cooperation, the gang members were acquitted, due to the unreliability of the evidence.

From a legal standpoint, that should have been the end of the matter. England had an established principle of "double jeopardy," which prevented suspects from being tried again, once acquitted, even in a private prosecution.

But for the Lawrences, the matter was far from over. According to Mrs. Lawrence, the trial simply indicated the breadth of the racism that resulted in Stephen's murder; it had been a sham:

> In my opinion, what happened in the Crown Court last year was staged. It was decided long before we entered the Courtroom what would happen—that the judge would not allow the evidence to be presented to the jury. In my opinion what happened was the way of the judicial system making a clear statement, saying to the black community that their lives are worth nothing and that the justice system will support anyone, any white person who wishes to commit a crime or even murder, against a black person. (Macpherson, 42.13)

Now, Mrs. Lawrence' statement was clearly over the top. It does not deny the sincerity of her emotions at the time to say that the proposition that British society would support the killing of any black person by any white person was contradicted by the zeal with which that very society had turned itself upside down in trying to bring the killers to justice, and indeed which elevated her statement to its importance. Whatever the motivations behind the extravagance of her assertion, whether they were political, psychological, or simply a penchant for hyperbole, they were certainly outside the limits of the sort of accuracy that a serious indictment of society should require.

Yet it was taken seriously indeed. Through its institutions, the society moved the accusation forward.

The next step was taken when the family brought the matter to the Police Complaints Commission, which authorized a major investigation by the Kent Constabulary. They produced a 400-page report which found that, while there were areas of the investigations that were of varying quality, there was not "any evidence to support allegations of racist conduct by police officers."

But things were not to remain at that stage. Rather, with the advent of the Labor government, a new inquiry was inaugurated under a panel headed by a retired High Court judge named Sir William Macpherson, which was intended to make recommendations concerning how the police should handle racially motivated crimes.

In the end, Macpherson (1999) produced a report running to 335 pages of text. Like the Kent Constabulatory, they found no evidence of overt racism or discriminatory behavior, either at the organizational level, regarding official policies, rules, or permitted practices that encouraged or condoned racism, or at the level of the conduct of individual police officers. Macpherson defined racism this way:

> 6.4 Racism in general terms consists of conduct or words or practices which disadvantage or advantage people because of their colour, culture, or ethnic origin.

He said: "We have not heard evidence of overt racism or discrimination, unless it can be said that the use of inappropriate expressions such as 'coloured' or 'negro' fall into this category." (6.3)

But they found the Police Service guilty of racism nonetheless. They did this by claiming that the Police Service was afflicted with "institutional racism," a term they derived from the American black power activists Stokely Carmichael and Charles V. Hamilton (1967). Moreover, through a breathtaking feat of generalization, they found it applied to the rest of British society as well.

I offer the view that it was this conclusion, which was widely cheered throughout the country, that was responsible for the subsequent trajectory of the British police.

This is Macpherson's definition of "institutional racism":

> The collective failure of an organisation to provide an appropriate and professional service to people because of their colour, culture, or ethnic origin. It can be seen or detected in processes, attitudes and behaviour which amount to discrimination through unwitting prejudice, ignorance, thoughtlessness and racist stereotyping which disadvantage minority ethnic people. (Macpherson, 6.34)

"Institutional racism" is a dangerous doctrine. If accepted, it means that the police force, and members of the police, cannot be trusted to control their own activities. They cannot be allowed to do what they do on the basis of having decided to do it, since any decision may contain prejudice, ignorance, or whatever, of which they are not aware.

Control of their activities must pass outside themselves to those who could make a charge of racism, and therefore invalidate whatever the police are doing. The viability of the police, therefore, must depend on the validity with which the charge is made. It is therefore necessary to see how such a charge might be grounded. What we can see in this critical and defining case is that it was not grounded in much.

In looking at the grounding of the charge, we need to note that this will be quite a trick, since, despite two monumental searches for it, no racism had been found. The Commission tried to make good that rather critical gap in two ways. First, they claimed the ability to read the organization's unconscious mind, as it were. In that way, it could assert the existence of racism, despite the failure to find any. But how could such a reading be done in a way that would establish their claim as firmly grounded?

Remarkably, in an issue of such importance, they did not try to ground it. They based their claims on "inference." But inference is a process of reasoning in which one moves from premises, according to explicit rules of derivation, to conclusion. Yet the movement is through logic alone. The conclusion has no more information than was present in the premises. It is only expressed in different form; unpacked, as it were. If one started off without racism, then, one could not wind up with it. But there was no racism in the premises; nor were rules of derivation given. Macpherson did not arrive at his accusations by inference. Their basis was only that he thought they were true (6.40). Essentially, they made the charges as dictum and defended them, not by reasoning, but by casting aspersions of racism on those who disagreed with them (e.g. 6.47). That hardly counts as firm grounding.

The second was to pass the attribution on to others. For example, they employed this definition of racism by the Association of Chief Police Officers: "any incident which included an allegation of racial motivation made by any person." Another, equivalently, was "any incident which is perceived to be racist by the victim or any other person." Thus, under this definition, something is racist if anybody says it is racist.

Why any other "other person" would be necessary to make the charge is unclear, since the Commission would, as another person, already have sufficient grounds to do so; and we have already noted the inadequacy of that.

In practice, this embarrassing lapse was covered over by granting special status to the victims of racism. But this was despite the fact that, in the absence of any other way to attribute such status, the designation of victimhood would be derived from the very accusation whose validity rested on the validity of that designation to begin with.

But this is classic *petitio principii*. It assumes what needs to be proved.

As far as the logic of demonstration goes, in this way the attribution becomes a tautology, a statement that is true by virtue of its terms alone. In Kant's terms, its truth is *a priori*.

But this definition deprives the designation of racism of any empirical content. It is unfalsifiable, in Popper's terms, and therefore incapable of being found false. But that also means that it is also incapable of being found, in any non-trivial sense, true. Anyone can accuse anyone else of racism, without accountability and for whatever reason, and that accusation itself would be all the proof necessary. The problem is that nothing of any significance will have been proved.

That, of course, does not mean that Mrs. Lawrence's claim, for example, was false. It simply means that if the claim were to be validated, it would have to be independently validated on the basis of evidence. But we have seen that no such evidence had been adduced, even within the testimony of the Lawrences. Their claim rested entirely on feeling. But add in the possibility that what was behind the charge was projection, or some other cognitive distortion, and we see that there was, in the Lawrence accusation, nothing that any court, or any group functioning as a court, and relying on objective evidence to ground its judgments, could have taken seriously.

The word for what is missing here is *proof*. The Macpherson Commission is operating within the tradition of British jurisprudence and it gets its credibility from that tradition. It is not a court, but it is a quasi-court. Its purpose is not to render a verdict, but its judgment will constitute a quasi-verdict. Yet the essence of that tradition is that conclusions are asserted as proved only when they are established by objective demonstration. The charges by the Lawrences were not proved through objective analysis, reason, and evidence, but rested entirely on feelings.

And yet, the Macpherson Commission accepted them.

We need to pause for a bit to consider what that means. The Commission knew the import of what it was doing. And it knew that, when it issued its finding of institutional racism, it was making an accusation that would have a profound effect on the way British society governed itself through its laws by protecting itself from lawlessness. Yet it made this charge anyway, despite lapses of reasoning that should have been obvious to anyone and that, I suggest, were, at some level, obvious to the Macpherson group itself.

How did they allow that to happen?

This is the point at which irrationality enters the list of matters that needs to be explained, and hence the point at which psychoanalytic theory suggests itself as useful. I therefore turn to the theory of political correctness and anti-Oedipal psychology that we have developed in this book to see what it can offer in the analysis of this otherwise strange behavior on the part of the Macpherson Commission.

In doing this, it is useful to confess that we are engaging in speculation here. Nothing I can offer will permit the level of proof that we have held the Commission delinquent for not delivering. On the other hand, we have no authority, or even quasi-authority, and the fate of the UK does not rest in our hands.

Mrs. Lawrence's Use of the Term "Racism"

The point I want to make is that, under the anti-Oedipal logic of political correctness, the term racism can come to mean something other than what we would have thought. Under the ordinary conception, the charge of racism appears to refer to something in the other, a pattern of behavior, perhaps, or a state of mind. Anti-Oedipal psychology opens the possibility that, in at least in some circumstances, it can be something quite different. Rather than being something in the other, it refers to something that is *not* in the other. What is not in the other is love for oneself.

Within the domain of the mother, the world would revolve around us with love. Fusion with her would mean the attainment of the ego ideal. We would be the center of a loving world. The normal self would be the pristine self.

Any response other than love would be experienced as a violation of the self, an assault upon the self. This would take specific form for those defined as oppressed, for instance those defined as having been oppressed because of their color. Lack of love would be seen as structured assault against the self on account of race; in other words, as racism.

Such violations would include indifference, which in this connection means treating people bureaucratically, with regard to general rules that do not attend to their individual subjectivity and their feeling of being important because they are who they are. This form of treatment is, of course, what gives bureaucracy a bad name. Often this name is well deserved; it is not, however, racism.

At any rate, recall that the premise here is that the father, the white, heterosexual male, has stolen the love. He can do whatever he wants to do and will be loved for it because he is who he is. His needs would be immediately granted. His self-justifications, his understandings of himself in relationship with others, will be automatically and unconditionally validated.

Holding this view, Mrs. Lawrence could easily conclude that if that love had not been stolen from her, those around her would validate her perspective, her self-justifications, and her understandings of herself in relationship with others. If they do not, it is because of the way she differs from the father, which in this case comes down to her race. Interestingly, that would include her belief that the reason her perspective is not validated is the racism of whoever does not grant that validation.

Political correctness, as we know, means that people defined as oppressed are entitled to love and idealization as compensation for the father's theft. The introduction of the issue of race then, invokes the basis of a person's claim of entitlement to love, of one's claim that the abuse of one's feelings by the indifference of the other was intolerable.

Our claim is that the finding of institutional racism by the Macpherson Commission consisted in an endorsement of this invocation. To demonstrate this, we will turn to the way the term "racism" was used in Macpherson's inquiry. In analyzing the thought of the Macpherson group, we have been guided by a superb book by Norman Dennis, George Erdos, and Ahmed Al-Shahi (2000, henceforth DEA) that rigorously and comprehensively dissects the Macpherson inquiry, with regard to its process and product.

The Macpherson group's report mentions five areas of evidence for the demonstration of racism: (a) the treatment of Mr. and Mrs. Lawrence at the hospital on the night of the murder, (b) the initial reaction to the victim and witness Duwayne Brooks, (c) the family liaison, (d) the failure of many officers to recognize Stephen's murder as a racially motivated crime, and (e) the lack of urgency and motivation in some areas of the investigation. (DEA, p. 36)

In evaluating their claims, it is important to recall again that none of the exhaustive investigations of the police found any concrete evidence of racism in any overt action or policy at all. The charges of racism, then, came down to nothing but feelings, and perhaps projections. Whatever they were, in the instances that are central to this case, they were made by the Lawrence family and Duwayne Brooks, and then ratified by Macpherson's group.

The crucial point about this is that, in agreement with our theory, in every case where racism was supposedly seen—as opposed to point (d), in which the evidence of racism was that it was *not* seen—racism referred to nothing other than treating the Lawrences and Brooks with indifference. This point is conclusively demonstrated by DEA. Considerations of concision preclude the enumeration of all these instances; three will serve as good enough illustrations.

The first bit of evidence considered by the Commission concerned a police officer named Little who was reported to have said to Mr. Lawrence at the hospital to which Stephen had been brought: "We've got a young lad in there, he is dead, we don't know who he is, but we would like to clarify that point. If it is not your son then all well and good, but we do need to know. I am sure you would like to know as well" (Macpherson, 12.44).

The Macpherson group observed, to begin with, that Mr. and Mrs. Lawrence required careful and sympathetic handling, and that Mr. Little's approach was insensitive and unsympathetic, which is true, but then they said this:

> Although he had worked in multi-cultural societies and areas throughout his service and believed that he treated everybody in the same way his lack of sensitivity and his inaction, particularly at the hospital, betrayed conduct which demonstrates inability to deal properly with bereaved people, and particularly those bereaved as a result of a terrible racist attack. He failed to deal with the family appropriately and professionally. This was unwitting racism at work. (Macpherson, 12.62)

The point is that there could have been any number of reasons for Officer Little's insensitivity. Maybe he was just an insensitive guy who would have treated anybody that way. Yet that possibility was not considered. Evidently, it was not thought to matter. The question is why such an obviously relevant issue was not taken into consideration. The reason, we suggest, is that it was actually not relevant to the way they were using the term "racism."

Our view is that, within anti-Oedipal psychology, race established a claim to maternal embrace; to being treated as the pristine self over and above the reasonable expectation that anyone would have regarding sensitive treatment. Anything short of that would be experienced, not as generalized insensitivity, but as a violation of the self on account of race, and hence as racism. Macpherson provided no substance to this vacuity, but simply carried it forward and gave it official blessing.

Another example here concerned the treatment of the Lawrences by a group of police who had been assigned as their liaison. From the point of view of the police, the main problem seemed to be that the case had become a lightning rod and, from the first day, had attracted a large number of racial activists, including, for various periods, the Anti-Racism League, the Black Panthers, and, most notably, a solicitor appointed by the Lawrences named Imran Khan, who specialized in cases related to race. They formed an entourage for the Lawrences and gave an antagonistic edge to the Lawrence's connections with the police.

Not surprisingly, such communications as took place were fraught. What is of interest to us, though, is that Mrs. Lawrence attributed the difficulty of this communication to racism.

Emblematic of this failure of communications was an incident in which Detective Constable Linda Holden brought to the Lawrences a hat and gloves that had been found near the scene of the crime and asked whether they belonged to Stephen. They responded that they were not his, and for DC Holden that was the end of the matter. For the Lawrences, it was not. They drew the implication that Holden was implying that Stephen was involved in a nefarious activity on the night of the murder, which they thought was racist. The Commission granted that such questioning was a routine part of police work, but they endorsed Mrs. Lawrence's accusation of racism, nonetheless.

On the whole, with regard to the failure of the liaison, the Commission recognized the potential for trouble, but put the onus entirely on the police. Their view was that the Lawrences were within their rights to arrange their circumstances in ways that seemed appropriate to them, within their cultures, and that it was understandable for them to be suspicious of the police. The police were responsible for dealing sensitively with any such circumstances to the point that no bad feelings could develop, and to anticipate and defuse all suspicions about their racism. If they did not, the reasonable suspicions of the Lawrences would be confirmed:

> 26.37 Plainly Mr & Mrs Lawrence were not dealt with or treated as they should have been. Their reaction and their attitude after their son's murder were those of a grieving family. The fact that they were in their eyes and to

> their perception patronised and inappropriately treated exhibits plain but unintentional failure to treat them appropriately and professionally within their own culture and as a black grieving family. DS Bevan and DC Holden will for ever deny that they are racist or that the colour, culture and ethnic origin of the Lawrence family played any part in the failure of family liaison. We are bound to say that the conclusion which we reach is inescapable. Inappropriate behaviour and patronising attitudes towards this black family were the product and a manifestation of unwitting racism at work. Coupled with the failure of the senior officers to see Mr & Mrs Lawrence and to sort out the family liaison we see here a clear example of the collective failure of the investigating team to treat Mr & Mrs Lawrence appropriately and professionally, because of their colour, culture and ethnic origin.

But the liaison officers were police, not social workers, and they were trained that way. In fact, since the nineteenth century, the British policing tradition, which has been the basis of professional policing throughout the West, has been defined by nine rules, originally laid down by Sir Robert (i.e., Bobby) Peale (see, e.g., CIVITAS n.d., no specific date). These rules, which give strong emphasis to the necessity of maintaining "public favour," are of particular interest to us here because they specify the paternal way public support has been sought. Rule Five is particularly relevant.

> 5. To seek and preserve public favour, not by pandering to public opinion; but by constantly demonstrating absolutely impartial service to law, in complete independence of policy, and without regard to the justice or injustice of the substance of individual laws, by ready offering of individual service and friendship to all members of the public without regard to their wealth or social standing.

In other words, the police have not been in the business of making specific groups feel loved, but of enforcing the law under the assumption that the laws are what they are, and applying them in the same way to everyone. The police, that is to say, operated within the framework of objective meaning provided by the paternal function.

The point is that the police were supposed to operate in this way in everything they did, whether there were circumstances of race or not. It would therefore be no more racist to operate this way regarding the Lawrences than it would be in the pure white precincts of the City of London.

From our point of view, what has happened here is that the Lawrences, in accordance with the politically correct ideology of the time, demanded maternal embrace. The police, although they actually tried as hard as they could, were not able to provide that. In the first place, being police, they were not in that business. Even the slightest lapse of the maternal function, like asking whether a hat and gloves belonged to Stephen, would be seized upon as validating the general anti-Oedipal case. But that did not keep the demand from being validated.

Yet, when we note that nothing remotely racial has been found in any of the lapses from the maternal embrace, this supports our proposition that the charge of racism has no racial content. The totality of the Lawrence's charges of racism is that, if they were white, they would have the maternal embrace

Another case in which Macpherson took standard police procedure to be racist developed from the fact that, among the police, the modal approach to the racial character of the crime was to acknowledge that it was racist, but to deny that, in accordance with the Lawrences' suspicions, it was *purely* racist. This, by itself, and with no further argument or introduction of relevant facts, was taken as proof of their racism.

This is a position that did not exist at the outset of the inquiry, but developed through it, and was a major factor in its conclusion. For example:

> 26.12 DS Bevan in common with other officers was not prepared to accept that the murder of Stephen Lawrence was purely a racist crime. It is difficult to understand how so many of the detectives working on this case were not willing to accept that this was so.

And:

> Expression of that view at the public Inquiry did nothing to encourage Mr & Mrs Lawrence or indeed the black community to revise or review their opinions of police officers.

Similarly:

> 19.44 Equally DS Davidson's attitude to the definition of this crime as racist or otherwise may well have affected his approach to the case. This is also clearly true of many other officers and in particular some of those close to him in the investigation whom he undoubtedly influenced. For example DC Budgen states that he regarded the murder as racist but changed his

> view subsequently to that expressed by DS Davidson. If officers expressed the view that they did not believe that the case was purely motivated by racism, when it so clearly was, then the perception of the black community in particular, and of all who heard the evidence at this Inquiry is inevitably that such an unjustifiable stance reflects inherent racism in the officers involved and in the police service.

And:

> DS Davidson and others have only themselves to blame for the perception that they were indeed "institutionally racist." This perception is justified in the sense that these officers approached the investigation in the wrong way and encouraged each other in their wrongful belief as to the motivation for the crime.

But aside from the fact that it was politically incorrect, there is no evidence given for saying that their way of approaching the crime was the wrong way. And if it so clear that the motivation for the crime was pure racism; so clear in fact that the police officers' failure to do was itself proof of their racism, how can it be that they, who were closest to the facts of the case, could have thought otherwise? It turns out they had good reason. For one thing, the gang had attacked a wide range of people, and even killed some, who were white.

PC Davidson testified:

> From other information I gleaned during the inquiry I would say that the persons … allegedly responsible were persons who would have killed anybody had they been there at the time. I do not think in my own mind that it was a race attack. I believe it was thugs attacking anyone, as they had done on previous occasions with other white lads. … They were thugs who were out to kill, not particularly a black person but anybody … not racism, just pure, bloody-minded thuggery. (Cathcart, *The Case of Stephen Lawrence* 1999, p. 351, cited in DEA, 80)

In fact, the racism of the attack was called into question by someone who had actually been there, one Royston Westbrook, a white man on his way home from work.

> He was at the bus stop with Stephen Lawrence, and witnessed the murder. As he got onto the bus which came almost at once he felt a shiver of appre-

> hension when he thought to himself that the attack seemed so motiveless that it might have been leveled at him if the two boys had not been there. (21.23)

The Commission does not accuse Mr. Westbrook of racism, but on the other hand they do not address the question of why a matter so clear was not clear to him as well. But so committed was the Commission to their view that they went so far as to withhold evidence of the gang's freewheeling, as opposed to racially focused, hatred in their public statement.

It turned out that during the period leading up to the private prosecution, the police had planted surveillance devices in the apartment used by some members of the gang. Nothing particularly useful to their case showed up, but in its Appendix, the Commission reported this exchange, in which the gang members are discussing a prize awarded in the National Lottery:

> *Norris*: [line blank]
> *Acourt*: Fifteen minutes.
> *Norris*: Why on earth do old grannies (want to play) they'll all die(tomorrow).
> *Acourt*: Good luck to them, fuck it.
> *Knight*: At least they are white.
> ('Transcript of compilation video IC/3', Macpherson, *The Stephen Lawrence Inquiry: appendices*, Cm 4262-II (Revised), Sequence 7)

What is present in the video, but which they do not report, which for me casts doubt on the integrity of their whole enterprise, is what followed:

> *Norris*: (*A little later*) See, if I was there, if I was one of the crowd, Itell you I would mug them.
> *Acourt*: What, rob them?
> *Norris*: If I was in a crowd, I tell you I'd fucking mug 'em, I'm telling you. For 500 grand … !
> *Acourt*: So would I, mate.
> *Norris*: … *I'd kill the cunts.* I'm telling you.
> *Acourt*: You've got to wait till they cashed it, gone to the bank
> (Cathcart, p. 234. cited in DEA, 74)

As DEA observe, "Mugging here is the language of money. Killing is the language of hate."

As against the view that this murder was a purely racist act, DEA (p. 75) offer this alternative perspective, based on Dennis (1993):

> The thuggish violence of the suspects was therefore broader than their racism, as it is among other children and youths like them being produced by British society—in numbers unmatched for at least 150 years (the period over which numbers have been available), and perhaps unmatched ever in British history.

And, we might add, which was also on display at the riots whose explanation this chapter is all about.

The case that the police reluctance to see the murder as pure racism as proof of their own racism is strained beyond the breaking point. But as DEA show, this is the standard form of reasoning in Macpherson's analysis. Its conclusion of racism was adopted, to repeat, in the absence of the slightest evidence that there was anything racial on the part of the police whatsoever, nor is there the slightest evidence to support the proposition, which one would think would be absolutely vital to Macpherson's case, that the police so charged would have acted any differently if the subject had been white.

What we have seen here is the Commission's wholesale adoption and validation of Mrs. Lawrence's perspective. But we have also seen that this adoption and validation was in violation of the most basic canons of proof, which we must believe that the Commission knew full well, and in an area of utmost consequence. We still need to understand, not only that the Commission adopted Mrs. Lawrence's view, but why they did so.

The Power of Political Correctness

Our claim has been that the abandonment by the Macpherson Commission of the canons of objective proof, and their endorsement of Mrs. Lawrence's subjective claims of racism was due to political correctness. But political correctness has two aspects, the psychological and the political.

We have seen the psychological power of political correctness throughout this book, and noted it to be the power of the primitive mother, the most powerful figure in the psyche.

This, however, is abstract. If we want to understand why the Macpherson Commission yielded, we have to have a sense of how, in this case, the power of the primitive mother was mobilized. What the Lawrence case offers is a case study of the generation of maternal power.

Mrs. Lawrence's initial statement to the Macpherson Commission gives us a concrete way of seeing what was going on in her mind. It is a very powerful document, and its power reveals much about the cause of the Commission's dereliction.

The Mother Versus the Machine

Mrs. Lawrence's statement, especially at the outset, is heartrending. Her story, compellingly told, is of a mother who is devastated by the murder of her beloved and totally innocent son, about whom the authorities do not appear to give a damn. For her, the world has been blown apart. For the police, this is just business as usual; just another killing in the big city.

One should have no doubt where a reader's sympathy will lie. And, one can have no doubt that if this tone carries forward, and Mrs. Lawrence increasingly feels abused by the indifference of the authorities, and rages against them, the odds are very good that she will carry the audience along with her.

What we have here is the generation of a powerful myth: the heroic mother standing up for the unique existence of her son against an official indifference that would just as soon consign him to the oblivion of his molecules. And the sympathies of every one of us, well aware of the tenuous, temporary, and resultantly absurd character of our own existences, will rally to her side. "Attention must be payed," we will say, in chorus with the words of Arthur Miller.

That is what happened and in a sense it is a testimonial to the best of what it means to be human that it did. But in the course of this how many of us will give ourselves over to considering the fact that, in order to be effective at keeping other equally unique individuals from being killed, a police force must learn how to do its work over time, and to bring the lessons it learns to bear through objective rules that are common to all the objects of its work, each of whom may feel, with perfect validity that, as far as their existential uniqueness is concerned, the organization does not give a damn?

This is the stuff of tragedy, or would be if we could wrap our heads around the whole thing. Typically we do not, however, and never more so than here. The comprehension of tragedy takes place in what Melanie Klein called the depressive position, in which others are seen as having both positive and negative aspects. However, in this case, splitting, the operation through which, in what she called the paranoid–schizoid position, good and bad are seen as separate and distinct, came to dominate.

The fundamental relevant fact was that Mrs. Lawrence was prone to thinking of the police as an essentially racist force that had no interest in solving crimes when the victims were black. On the contrary, she would come increasingly to the belief that the police were the bad object, at best getting in the way, at worst siding with the killers, and protecting them. Moreover, not only was it the police force, it was British society itself.

The effect of this was to redefine the myth from mother against the machine to mother against British society. British society bought the redefinition of this myth. The effect was to redefine the dynamics of her case. Instead of being the drama of mother against the machine, played before the audience of British society, British society joined in on her side as a co-participant, and the social process became British society against itself.

This helps us understand the peculiar behavior of the Macpherson Commission. As an elite institution, they held the combined role of being both the representative of British society, seen as evil, and its defender against evil. How they would handle this is by designating a part of the society to bear the evil, and then defending against that evil in the name of the rest of society, by which essentially they meant themselves. In effect, they set up a scapegoat. The name of the scapegoat was the British police.

I want to show how this myth developed through an analysis of Mrs. Lawrence's testimony.

Mrs. Lawrence's Story

Beginning on the day after Stephen's killing, political forces committed to the condemnation of the police on account of their supposed racism, most notably the Anti-Racist Alliance, descended on the Lawrences' house and made themselves at home. After a while, she recognized that they had their own agendas and distanced herself from them, but they had their impact on her way of seeing things, as she acknowledges, helping to determine that she would see the police' treatment of her son as part of a general pattern.[1] This would lead to the transformation of her role from that of the mother who was concerned with justice for her son, to political warrior.

The political role that Mrs. Lawrence took was essentially maternal; she defined the maternal role as political. We may say that she became a political mother, which meant that the maternal would operate at the level of the world. The central idea was that the world would be brought to love her son. Stephen Lawrence should be the center of a loving world, and her function as a mother was to make that happen.

Consider this:

> There was then an invitation to meet President Mandela. We went because we saw him as a way of highlighting the fact that the British government and the people in power here were not interested, and that nobody had come to visit us except for the local MP, Peter Bottomley. I remember saying to him during the week of the murder: "Does the Prime Minister know about my son?" He said, "Well, I don't think so." I said: "Why not?" and he couldn't answer. (Lawrence 1998)

But, of course, individual murders, of which there were 565 in the UK in 1993 (Murder UK 2015), are not typically attended to by the Prime Minister. And the visit of the local Member of Parliament is hardly consistent with the idea that nobody in power was interested.

Similarly, recalling that the murder had taken place on the Thursday night:

> Nobody was showing an interest that a young man had been killed and that the papers, even though they ran the story, there was nothing on the Friday, but they ran the story on the Saturday. Then you had the London bombing and that was it, no more mention of Stephen. (*ibid*)

Fusion of infant and mother works both ways. Stephen being the center of the world means that she is the world. What goes along with this is omnipotence, taking the form of grandiosity. She is clearly of the view that she should be, if not running the investigation, at least a dominant element in it.

Specifically, Mrs. Lawrence says that she was receiving information all the time and that she passed this information, which is to say rumors, on to the police. In her view, they should have taken this "information" and used it to arrest the thugs. Her omnipotence guaranteed the adequacy, or at least the crucial importance, of this information. Anything less, she believed, could only be due to racism:

> Once the information started coming in through the questions, it was the question following: "Why has no one been arrested?" It started dawning on

me that, if it had been the other way around that night, somebody would have been arrested, regardless of whether they had done it or not.

The point is that there was a blurring in her mind between the information that she had supplied, and which the police had from the same and other sources, and the fact that she had supplied it. Any minimization of her information was taken as a personal assault:

> Before the meeting with the police I remember being concerned that although they had all the information that had been sent from us, from my own mind I decided to write down the names, so I got the book, I wrote all the names on a piece of paper and I took it with me. … I handed the paper to Illsley. I don't know why I handed it to him … I remember sitting very quiet listening to what was happening around me and watching Illsley, having given him the paper, to see what he was doing. That's when I saw him fold the paper up so small and I think on that meeting—I don't think I said anything because it was too much of a shock. He rolled the piece of paper up in a ball in his hand. I was so shocked by what I saw.

Note that Illsley already had, from her if not from elsewhere, the information on the piece of paper.

The main theme of her account is that all she wanted was information and the police were not forthcoming. It is clear, however, that she wanted only certain kinds of information: she wanted to be told that they were doing what she thought they should be doing, that they were succeeding, and that she was instrumental in that success.

> Illsley … patronised me—as if I cannot think for myself. It was a constant argument with him. He would never give a straight answer to my questions. I was getting frustrated because I was asking simple questions and if they had ever said, "This is what's happening, we have arrested so and so, it was as a result of the names you gave us, this where we are at and we are moving from here to there." I would have been satisfied. That was all I was asking for.

Out of this frustration arose her adoption of a political role:

> As the week progressed I was getting more and more angry because nothing was happening. We were not told anything. Nobody was being arrested and it just dawned on me at the time that they had no intention of doing anything about Stephen's murder and that's when I started taking an active

> role at the meetings with Philpot. Ros and Carl were there, I think because they were members of the community and because Ros is a worker from the Greenwich Racial Equality Unit

The orientation toward racial politics only deepened as time went by.

> When we started our series of meetings with senior officers things did not get much better. I have seen references to our "thirst" for information which I frankly find offensive. This was after all the murder of our son. It was also claimed that the police found dealing with our solicitor a hindrance. Basically we were seen as gullible simpletons. This is best shown by Illsley's comment that I had obviously been primed to ask question. Presumably there is no possibility of me being an intelligent black woman with thoughts of her own who is able to ask questions for herself. We were patronised and fobbed off. As the meetings went on I got more and more angry. I thought the purpose of the meetings was to give us progress reports. But what actually happened was they would effectively say, "Stop questioning us, we are doing everything." That simply wasn't true and it led me to believe then and now they were protecting the suspects.

It needs to be said that, as a matter of procedure, and as acknowledged by the Commission, the police would want to limit the information that got out, and that would tend to limit the amount of information made available to the Lawrences. At the same time, the increasing politicization by the Lawrences could not have increased the police's desire to be more forthcoming:

> The police were not interested in keeping us informed about the investigation. We were simply regarded as irritants. … DAC Osland … said that if we persisted in accusing the officers of being racist he would recommend that they could sue us. I now see in briefing notes that in July 1993 he said that he was "fed up to the back teeth with the Lawrence family."

Mrs. Lawrence's belief in the efficacy of her information arose from her omnipotence, not from a realistic sense of what it would take to convict people in the context of the law and, especially, its rules of evidence. Thus:

> The information that I was getting, instead of passing it on to the police I should have gone and made a citizen's arrest myself. Then there would have been no need to waste time and taxpayer's money now on an Inquiry because the guilty would be behind bars.

And her ignorance of the legal framework in which the police operated, not to mention her lack of concern for it, could easily have led to patronization, and that without the slightest intrusion of racism. Here is another incident in which the application of the objective rules is taken as racism:

> Illsley believed that we were primed beforehand that we were told what sort of questions to ask and how to ask them. There was one incident that has stuck out in my mind when I was asking about the boys in prison. I was asking why couldn't they not put a bug in with them in the room to listen to what was being said, because if they would not talk to the police they would talk to individuals, and Illsley said "We do not do things like this—no way" and I could remember that he was very angry because he assumed I was told to ask that question.

But although she believes Illsley is angry because he assumes she has been told to ask the question, she has no direct evidence of that. Neglected is the possibility that he is indignant about being asked to do something contrary to police policy.

The tension between objectivity and Mrs. Lawrence's subjectivity came to the fore in the private prosecution, where there was a directed verdict of not guilty, based on the inadequacy of the evidence. Mrs. Lawrence was devastated by her lack of efficacy and took the whole process as corrupt on the grounds of race:

> From the first day in Court I could sense that things were going wrong from the time the Judge sat down. It was as though we were just pawns, being played, we had no say. We had no part of it, we had nothing to do with what was being directed. We were just being swept along. It was like watching a play where someone is behind the screen being a puppet and someone pulling the strings. You think you are in charge yet you are not. You are led to believe that you have a say. I think after the committal I thought we were getting somewhere and we are going to prove that this is what the CPS should have done and achieve what they should. After the collapse at the Old Bailey I realised there was no way that the State would have allowed us to have done that, because that would have been a slap in the face for the Government and the Crown Prosecution Service. What was coming across for me at the time was—"Who do we think we are—some black family telling them that their justice system stinks."

If not racism, what could the failure of the whole project have been due to?

I believe the Kent (Police Complaints Authority) Report "has not got to the bottom of what went on. It's scratched the surface." At the beginning it was saying that the police officers were not racist in their attitude and behaviour towards the case, but clearly by the end of it their actions show there has to be some reason. If it was not racism what was it? Incompetence? Corruption? That only goes some way to explain. We are told that these officers have years of experience at investigating murder so this was not new to them. What when wrong? Something did. Their attitude tells me it was racism. Police have a pre-conceived idea of what black people are like, and their behaviour demonstrates this yet again. According to my understanding the only regular dealings police have with black families is when they are criminals. So, coming across a black family who have no criminal background is new to them—an alien concept. It was like you have to be a criminal if you are black.

Racism is institutionalised. From what I have read in the PCA report it's like "How dare you think I am racist." Well I say—how dare I think you are not, because nothing in your actions has proven to me that you are not, and I see no other explanation for your attitude and behaviour.

I believe because the police spent so much time investigating my family and Stephen they came to the conclusion that we were not criminals and so they had no case. They were trying to prove that Stephen was involved in something and was not attacked just for being black.

Bringing the matter to the Macpherson Inquiry:

What I want from this Inquiry is to show the police's behaviour and their inaction. Through their negligence these people have been allowed to walk free, and through the legal system three of the boys can never be brought to justice. I believe the police had a hand in the whole thing.

Every officer who has come in has made matters worse. When you list the catalogue of errors you have to ask yourselves whether there possibly can be so many mistakes or whether they must be deliberate acts. By keeping us occupied they kept the black community quiet, it gave us a false sense of security and it made black people feel that justice could be achieved. We now know after the Kent Inquiry just how much had gone wrong and how much should have been done that wasn't and we are discovering more everyday.

And in conclusion, returning to the origin:

> I would like Stephen Lawrence to be remembered as a young man who had a future. He was well loved and had he been given the chance to survive, maybe he would have been the one to bridge the gap between black and white because he didn't distinguish between black and white. He saw people as people.

What we have, in sum, is a concatenation. On one hand, we have the mother fighting for justice for her son. She has become iconic, and has drawn the sympathies of a whole nation. On the other, we have a bureaucracy, a father, that has not been able to deliver that justice, and whose failure Mrs. Lawrence sees as racism. Mrs. Lawrence, then, is drawing British society into condemnation of itself. Inevitably, this takes the form of a broad and powerful condemnation of its elites.

To understand the farcical reasoning of the Macpherson Commission, therefore, I suggest that Mrs. Lawrence, with her huge and powerful following has created a question for these elites. And the question is "How can we shut this woman up?"And their answer was that they would sacrifice the police; they would throw the police overboard.

Because of their defining procedures, they were incapable of defending themselves. They therefore needed to move outside of their procedures, but without it appearing they had done so. It seems they were forced into doubletalk, to smoke and mirrors, to the illogical that appears to be logic. This doubletalk was the Macpherson Report.

The purpose of the doubletalk was to set up the police to bear the wrath of Mrs. Lawrence and her followers in British society, through the nonsensical designation of institutional racism.

Ironically, from this point of view, we can see that the charge of institutional racism made a certain kind of perverse sense. Doing what the police had traditionally done, even if they did it in perfect concordance with their ideals, would be seen as racist.

In effect, the police had emerged from the Inquiry with their identity having been spoiled. They could no longer respond as police because that identity had been stigmatized. They were required to turn their aggression inward against their own enforcement of the laws, instead of expressing their aggression outwards in the process of law enforcement. Acting as police would conflict with the politically correct injunction to love the oppressed.

From that point onwards, the police could not know what they were supposed to do. The injunction placed upon the police was not, as in the Peale principles, to ignore public opinion, but to be sensitive and even subordinate to it. And the principle which directed their sensitivity was based on the premise that, left to themselves, they would be seen as racist, which is now implied by the equal enforcement of the laws. Henceforth, relying on the laws as given would make the police vulnerable to a charge of racism, confirming their badness. Under these circumstances, the option of essentially withdrawing from the situation and doing nothing would be preternaturally appealing.

At the same time, given the supposed racism of the police, the oppressed would naturally feel that objective treatment is an entirely illegitimate violation of the self, and would be absolved of the necessity to turn their own aggression inward as guilt. It would be free to flow outward in the form of riot. And that riot would be largely unconstrained by the forces of social order.

Conclusion

As with all great empires, the foundation and highest achievement of the British was positive law: the paternal function. The question is why they could not defend it.

My suggestion here is that the British elite had a choice, given the politics of this situation. They could defend positive law, or they could defend themselves. In choosing to sacrifice the paternal function, in the form of the police, they chose to defend themselves, not recognizing that, in doing so, they had given up their own legitimacy.

So they would live to rule another day, but they would rule, not as fathers, but only as men, and only as vassals of the primitive maternal.

It was as a lineal development of this that they would issue, on the day of the riots, as well as before, the condemnation of society that would leave the rioters free to express their aggression, and put a damper on the aggression of the police. We have seen the consequences of that. We should not be surprised if, in one form or another, we see them again.

Note

1. "With hindsight you need groups like ARA to point out issues to you because someone like myself was not aware that this sort of thing was happening on a daily basis. We did not continue with their support because we felt they had an agenda. They said they were there for the family but they were there to highlight ARA and they weren't taking the family's feelings into consideration. They saw this as something to push themselves forward and to make themselves better known." (Lawrence 1998: STATEMENT OF DOREEN LAWRENCE—8th March 1998, Appendix 6).

References

Carmichael, S., and C.V. Hamilton. 1967. *Black Power: The Politics of Liberation in America*. Harmondsworth: Penguin.

Carter, Helen. 2011. Rioter Profile: 'I thought of it as like a battle, like a war'. *The Guardian*, December 5. http://www.guardian.co.uk/uk/2011/dec/05/rioter-profile-battle-like-war.

Cathcart, Brian. 1999. *The Case of Stephen Lawrence*. New York: Viking.

CIVITAS: The Institute for the Study of Civil Society. n.d. Principles of Good Policing. http://www.civitas.org.uk/pubs/policeNine.php.

Dennis, Norman. 1993. Rising Crime and the Dismembered Family. London: IEA Health and Welfare Unit. pp. 1–3.

Dennis, Norman, George Erdos, and Ahmed Al-Shahi. 2000. *Racist Murder and Pressure Group Politics*. London: Institute for the Study of Civil Society.

Freud, Sigmund. 1962. *Civilization and its Discontents*. First American edition. Trans. and ed. James Strachey. New York: Norton.

Lawrence, Doreen. 1998. Statement of Doreen Lawrence. The Stephen Lawrence Inquiry: Report of an Inquiry by Sir William Macpherson of Cluny, Home Office, Cm 4262-I, February. http://www.archive.official-documents.co.uk/document/cm42/4262/sli-ap6.htm and http://www.archive.official-documents.co.uk/document/cm42/4262/sli-ap6a.htm.

Lewis, Paul. 2011. A Fire Lit in Tottenham that Burned Manchester: The Rioters' Story. *The Guardian*, December 4.

Macpherson, Sir William. 1999. The Stephen Lawrence Inquiry: Report of an Inquiry by Sir William Macpherson of Cluny, Home Office, Cm 4262-I, February. http://www.archive.official-documents.co.uk/document/cm42/4262/4262.htm.

Murder UK. 2015. UK Murder Statistics. Murder UK: Documenting and Investigating Murder in the UK. http://www.murderuk.com/misc_crime_stats.html.

Riots Communities and Victims Panel. 2011. 5 Days in August: An Interim Report on the 2011 English Riots. 28 November, p. 69. http://riotspanel.independent.gov.uk/wp-content/uploads/2012/04/Interim-report-5-Days-in-August.pdf.

———. 2012. The final report of the Riots Communities and Victims Panel. 28 March. http://riotspanel.independent.gov.uk/wp-content/uploads/2012/03/Riots-Panel-Final-Report1.pdf.

Rusbridger, Alan, and Judith Rees. 2011. *Reading the Riots: Investigating England's Summer of Disorder—Full Report*. London: The Guardian and the London School of Economics. 14 December.

Schwartz, Howard S. 2003. *Revolt of the Primitive: An Inquiry Into the Roots of Political Correctness*. Piscataway, NJ: Transaction Publishers.

——— 2010. *Society Against Itself: Political Correctness and Organizational Decay*. London: Karnac.

CHAPTER 7

What was the Occupy Wall Street Protest a Protest of?

Introduction

"History," it has been said, "does not repeat itself, but it rhymes." To a former sixties radical, specifically myself, the Occupy Wall Street (OWS) protest had an uncanny quality. On one hand, it looked rather similar to what we used to do back then, but at the same time there were elements that were importantly discordant.

I satisfied myself on the similarities by a trip to Zucotti Park a few weeks after the protest began. Aside from the fact that they set up their habitation much better than we ever did, the ambience was quite familiar. Earnest, informal, no indicators of status, clear belief in the importance of what they were doing, and so on.

The people certainly looked similar to the demonstrators of the sixties; in fact, many of them appeared to be the same. I looked around for friends, but could not find any.

But differences were also apparent, and widely noted. These were often put by saying that the Occupy group had no demands. That was something that certainly was not said about my generation. And it raises the possibility that the changes may be profound indeed.

It cannot help but be significant that OWS not only acknowledges this lack of demands, but also embraces it, taking it as a virtue. What they are demanding is so comprehensive that no specific set of demands can come

H.S. Schwartz, *Political Correctness and the Destruction of Social Order*, DOI 10.1007/978-3-319-39805-1_7

together to present it. For example, Judith Butler, writing in Tidal #1 (2011), says:

> To demand justice is, of course, a strong thing to do. It also involves every activist in a philosophical question: What is justice, and what are the means through which the demand for justice can be made? The reason it is said that sometimes there are "no demands" when bodies assemble under the rubric of "Occupy Wall Street" is that any list of demands would not exhaust the ideal of justice that is being demanded.

The problem is that this is so idealized and generalized that it offers no guidance to the task of social reorganization that we would think the movement would be about.

I submit that it is in this gap between the derisory dismissal of specific demands and the idealized generalizations that can provide no guidance to action that OWS' unique character lies. For no one is really asking them for specific demands.

What they are being asked for is a framework of understanding that would *give significance* to demands. What they lack, in other words is not so much demands, but a *theory of organization*: a systematic comprehension of the way social systems operate, which could give rise to a program of action, comprehensible within that framework, that could be expected to result in a situation that is better than the present conditions that they find so unacceptable. Within that context, demands would represent intermediate steps, or way stations, on the road to a final goal. They would thus represent the concrete embodiment of the program. Demands, then, define what the group means by moving forward. Lack of demands suggests that the group has no idea of what forward motion would consist in.

Ultimately, I will try to show that the absence of a theory of organization, on the level of society or any other, is not a matter of happenstance. It is not as if they have just not gotten around to coming up with one. Rather, the ideological core of OWS makes a theory of organization, impossible; in fact, it is directed against the very idea of organization. But that is an idea that will take time to unfold.

In the meantime, we may note that is in this lack of a theory of organization that we can see the difference between the OWS and the protests of the sixties. For during the sixties, a theory of society, in the form of Marxist class analysis, broadly and paradigmatically speaking, was entirely evident, and led to a more or less concrete program of action that promised to bring about a reformulation of social order that would satisfy the highest levels of idealism. The problem was, of course, that this program of action, exhaustively tried all over the world, led to disastrous results that could not be concealed from anyone.[1] Its failure led, if not to a universal discrediting of Marxian understanding, then at least to its dispatch to marginal quarters.

Yet, something like it has shown up at Zucotti Park; a rhyme of some kind. But what can it be?

Slavoj Žižek, (2011) in a piece in *The Guardian* called Occupy First, Demands Come Later, wrote:

> In a kind of Hegelian triad, the western left has come full circle: after abandoning the so-called "class struggle essentialism" for the plurality of anti-racist, feminist, and other struggles, capitalism is now clearly re-emerging as the name of the problem.
>
> In a word, the critique of capitalism has become again the ideological basis of the western left.

The problem is that "capitalism," for the left, was defined by class analysis: private ownership of the means of production and a proletariat whose only place in the system derived from its "labor power." Labor constituted the only source of value, so profit could only be the expropriation of surplus value from the input of labor. Enterprises producing the same commodities are necessarily in competition with each other which necessarily generates a competition for greater profits that can only be addressed by cutting back on the wages of labor, immiserating the working class. But the working class, like the slave in Hegel's master–slave dialectic, is the only one that does anything and therefore the only one that knows how to do what is done. In this arrangement they are in a position to overthrow the capitalist class, which is parasitic and contributes nothing, and reorganize their labor to satisfy their own interests and desires.

Putting the matter that way yields a reasonably clear program consisting in organizing the workers, by which can be meant any group who are lower down in a hierarchy, for revolution, which refers to a seizure of power from the ruling class and a reorganization of society in the interest of the workers. This strategy follows from the theoretical framework and gives significance to the program and its demands, which connect specific realities with the ideals that are sought.

In other words, understanding capitalism within the context of Marx' theoretical understanding already implicitly defines a program for establishing its replacement.

The flaw here is one that should be visible to any educated person. Marx' theory had no way of understanding the extraordinarily capacity of capitalism to use the imagination. For once creativity became a basis for competition then wages would be set on the basis of marked individual differences in contributions. The necessity to continually lower wages for everyone, based on the idea of labor as a commodity, would be thoroughly obviated. This fact of life, made unavoidable by the sclerosis and stagnation of the Soviet Union, undermined the capacity of class analysis to be taken seriously.

From this, it is easy enough to see where the problem is for OWS. The collapse of class theory meant that the term "capitalism" was deprived of its native context for meaning. It had lost its capacity to serve as a basis for demands and for a program, generally. But that capacity was the reason for its appeal. The question is, what is the critique of capitalism without the Marxist theory of class struggle?

The assault upon capitalism is clearly in evidence at OWS and on the left, but the question is what does it mean? How is it to be understood? If it cannot serve as a basis for a program, how is it serving? And what does it say about the left, as an element of contemporary culture, that it is still in a position of such significance?

To get a handle on these questions, I will examine what OWS has in mind by the term "capitalism." We know at the outset that a conscious theory is not on offer, but an exploration of the unconscious dynamics may tell us something about the potential for this cultural movement and about the nature of work and organization that this potential contains.

The Question of Capitalism

As we know, the OWS protest defined itself as being against "capitalism." Our question now is what does that term mean to them?

We think of capitalism as an economic system, representing a specific way of organizing objective reality. Its elements are the private ownership of the means of production, wage labor, and so on. But objective definitions of capitalism are rarely encountered in the self-expressions of

OWS. In fact, economic parameters hardly appear at all, much less as focal points of criticism.

This does not necessarily go with the territory. Protest movements based on Marxism, for example, rely on what Marx put forward as a scientific, empirical, and objective theory about the nature of capitalism. Within that theory, the normal workings of the capitalist economic system would lead inexorably to the system's demise. One may think well or ill of the theory he offered, but there can be no doubt that it was intended to be an objective understanding of its subject matter. And one can be in no doubt that the revolutionary communist movements to which it gave rise, beginning with the Bolsheviks, incorporated that presumption (see, e.g., the writings of Lenin). Yet in the protest movements of today, most notably the Occupy movement, these kinds of objective, theoretical considerations are absent.

This raises a question. If we take it for granted that the focus of these protest movements is capitalism, but they are not thinking of it objectively as an economic system, how are they thinking of it? In other words, what are these critics, in their own minds, critics of? What does capitalism mean to them?

To answer that question, I looked at some of the written material produced by OWS. I looked at their expressions of what they are about, particularly in the form of the documents posted in their name at the websites http://occupytheory.org/ and, more selectively, at http://www.adbusters.org/, which is the website for Adbusters, the magazine that initiated OWS.

In an exercise of this sort, one quickly comes to the question of whether specific material is central to the issue one is trying to understand, or peripheral to it. In this case, that distinction becomes especially difficult to make because OWS was seized upon by a variety of political groups, generally on the left, each with its own ideology, who attempted to co-opt OWS and bring it into their orbit. It was therefore presented through a range of political perspectives.

I am going to suggest, however, that there was an underlying idea that could be said to represent the characteristic perspective of OWS and through which we can recognize a specific identity.

I will look at the meaning of capitalism within the context of the way OWS has of the world and of itself within it. I will argue that, insofar as OWS is directed against capitalism, capitalism, as they understand it, is not an economic system; a way of arranging objective reality. For them, reality is not objective, but moral; capitalism stands for a character in a morality play.

Using psychoanalytic theory, I am going to try to understand this character. My conclusion will be that what they have in mind is society as such, and specifically the psychic configuration that makes society possible, what Lacan calls the paternal function.

First Approximation

Looking at their documents and trying to understand what they are against, a number of things come to mind. First is that the focus is very diffuse. The term capitalism is often used by those who identify with the movement and are recognized by it as one of themselves, such as Žižek (2012), who addressed the General Assembly (GA) and then built that address into a book. But, as I said, it is generally not used to denote a clearly defined economic system, and nothing else takes a place that would anchor a specific meaning. Hence the meaning of the term varies broadly. Along the same lines, capitalism is rarely seen as something standing by itself, with an existence independent of the way people feel about it, as an economic system would. Rather, it is typically seen as an instrument, a way of affecting the world through which some very bad people operate.

Who those people are is, again, designated broadly. They are referred to, of course, as the capitalists, but also as the 1 %, the bankers, Wall Street, the bosses, financial capitalists, millionaires and billionaires, and so on. The products of the use of this system by these bad people are immoral conditions that are also specified broadly: injustice, oppression, inequality, and so on. But however their focus is specified, and at whatever level, one thing that is constant is the idea of its malevolence. Indeed, it is seen, not just as a malevolent force, but as a force that is malevolent in its essence.

It therefore makes sense to consider the object of their protest as something that relates to the capitalist economic system in some way that is structurally undefined and is not capable of being expressed with an objective definition. It is not by happenstance that it is controlled by bad people and does bad things; that is its defining characteristic. Its essence, that is to say, is moral. We must give it a name. We'll call it the Thing.

For psychoanalysis, the Thing represents a "bad object." Its essence is to be bad. That is not to say that it does not do anything good, but only that when it does something good, it has been forced to do so by good forces, as when the 99 % force changes in the law that benefit the people.

Since a bad object arises from splitting, there must be a good object in the neighborhood. Of course there is, and it consists in the movement of which they are part, which they idealize exhaustively. Within the context of their movement, they are loved for being who they are and are free to do whatever expresses who they are. This extends to their various manifestations, most importantly their General Assemblies, which serve as their collective discussion venue and decision making function. The GA, with its lack of hierarchy, its inclusiveness, and its collective spontaneity, is taken as a prefiguration of the hoped for future, in which it will function as a structural element (e.g., Hardt and Negri 2012).

As a good object, this movement is in essential opposition to the bad object, which is capitalism as a first approximation, but is actually something deeper, which we call the Thing. We'll now try to get a handle on the meaning of the Thing, taking into consideration its unconscious as well as its conscious elements.

What is the Thing?

Scenario One: Communique #1

As an expression of what the protestors are against, one bit of writing stands out from the others; one that cannot be the product of co-optive forces. This is an unsigned document,[2] (Anonymous, 2011) amounting to a manifesto, entitled *Communiqué#1*, which appears on the website occupytheory.org as the lead piece in Issue 1 of a publication called *Tidal: Occupy Theory, Occupy Strategy* dated December 2011. I will quote from it extensively.

It begins:

> We were born into a world of ghosts and illusions that have haunted our minds our entire lives. These shades seem more alive to us than reality, and perhaps by some definition are more actual, hyper-real. We grew up in this world of screens and hyperbole and surreal imagery, and think nothing of a long-dead actor appearing on a wall in our homes to urge us to buy or live a certain way.

> We have no clear idea how life should really feel … We sense something is wrong only through the odd clue.

In this, they find themselves different from most of the people around them:

> Some generations ago, we might have all been burned, perhaps rightly, as witches. After all, who knows where these images really come from?
>
> We notice a vague spiritual nausea, hard to discuss in a world where most serious, hard-working people have little time to believe in the existence of the soul. The ghosts that come to us offer no vocabulary to describe the emptiness they helped create within us.

They associate this "world of screens and hyperbole and surreal imagery" with advertising, but this is a metaphor for the whole setting in which they live. Their lives, that is to say, are ordered by these images, and are therefore controlled by the economic forces within which the images play their parts, and by Wall Street, the people they see controlling those forces, who make use of them for their own nefarious purposes:

> At Wall Street we see that the basic quantum of experience has become the transaction; that life's central purpose is to convert all of existence into tradable currency.

And

> It all seems to be of a part: the images crowding in on us as cheap and lifeless as the products they represent, built in factories owned by hollow men trying to fill their emptiness with mansions and treasures that they drained from us. In so doing they make the rest of the world as dark and dead as they are.

But they are having none of it:

> We have come here to doubt and to dispute that plan.

And:

> We have come to Wall Street as refugees from this native dreamland, seeking asylum in the actual. That is what we seek to occupy. We seek to rediscover

> and reclaim the world … We have come here to vanish those ghosts; to assert our real selves and lives; to build genuine relationships with each other and the world; and to remind ourselves that another path is possible.

"Another path is possible," but what would it consist in? Our protestors offer little specific direction, but a general principle is evident. They will "assert our real selves and lives," and "build genuine relationships with each other and the world." These are presumably the opposite of the world they find themselves in.

The only reality that stands outside these fictions consists in the residues of our childhoods, before we got caught up in the system. These are who we really are, and the protestors have gathered at Wall Street to reclaim their real selves and to build a new world based on authentic relationships with real others.

Reading *Communique #1* reminded me very strongly of a film that appeared in 1999 (Wachowski and Wachowski) called The Matrix. I rented it and watched it.

Scenario Two: The Matrix

In this film,[3] the main protagonist is a computer programmer named Thomas Anderson, who is told by his employer that he has "a problem with authority" and had better get with the program. But Anderson also has a clandestine identity as a hacker named Neo. He is contacted by a group of outlaws, led by a man called Morpheus, who reveal to him that the world in which he thinks he lives is an artificial framework of illusion called the Matrix. It was created by machines who originally were the outgrowth of Artificial Intelligence, but who came to dominate the humans who had created them. The actual humans spend their lives in pods, with tubes and cables leading in and out. They are senseless to their actual surroundings, their minds kept engaged in the illusions that they think are their lives. In fact, they are nothing but a source of energy for the machines. Morpheus explains:

> What is the Matrix? Control. The Matrix is a computer generated dream world, built to keep us under control in order to change a human being into this. [Morpheus holds up a battery to Neo]

The outlaws are the only ones who live in reality, and Neo chooses to join them, for no other reason than the pursuit of the truth.

Reality, which Morpheus refers to as "the desert of the real," turns out to be a very grim and barren place, entirely without amenities. The humans, in an early attempt to deprive the machines of energy have polluted the sky. The world is now so cold that humans can live only underground, near the earth's core, where there is heat. Everything is ugly. The food is tasteless and monotonous. Aside from the technical and physical prowess they have developed, the outlaws do not appear to have anything except the truth and their own relationships to each other.

The only meaning their lives seem to possess is given by their struggle to defeat the machines and free the humans from their illusions, a task that has hitherto been impossible since the hegemony of the Matrix is defended by a powerful, interchangeable, group of "Agents" named Smith, Jones, and Brown. In addition to their coercive power they have also the argument that the Matrix is the real reality, in addition to being far more appealing. This argument was sufficient to persuade one of the outlaws, a man whose outlaw name is Cipher, who betrays the group.

Morpheus is captured by the outlaws, but in the end is rescued by a heavily armed Neo, now recognizing himself as The One who is destined to save humanity. In the movie's ultimate scene he directs a message to the forces of the machines:

> Neo: I know you're out there … I can feel you now. I know that you're afraid. You're afraid of us, you're afraid of change … I don't know the future … I didn't come here to tell you how this is going to end, I came here to tell you how this is going to begin. Now, I'm going to hang up this phone, and I'm going to show these people what you don't want them to see. I'm going to show them a world without you … a world without rules and controls, without borders or boundaries. A world … where anything is possible.

Comparing the Thing and the Matrix

The reason the Thing reminded me of the Matrix is clear. As metaphors, they are essentially the same, and it is on the level of metaphor, emotional reality, where their importance is located. In both cases, most people live in a world of created illusions, which are deliberately created by malevolent others. In one case these others are "hollow men," "dark and dead." In the other they are machines. In neither case do these others have any regard for the human beings whose lives they control through these illusions, which they have created to serve their own purposes. Their purpose in one case is to use the humans as a source of energy, as batteries. In the other, which may also be considered a source of energy, the purpose is to use the people to keep the system moving through production and consumption, in order to "fill their emptiness with mansions and treasures that they drained from us."

But in both cases there is a band who have broken free of these illusions and lives in reality. They have returned to their authentic identities and are members of a group who share the collective purpose of rescuing the people from their illusions. The free people aim to defeat the dominating others, but in the interim their existences are stark and difficult. Their only rewards are the authentic relationships among them and the sense of purpose that they gain from their struggle. The terms in which this story is put differ, but the emotional correlate is the same.

Those are the similarities. But there are also differences. The most important difference is that one of them is an economic system, the other is not; the Matrix is a power plant. The importance of this, I suggest, is that it reveals that the Occupy movement is *not essentially an attack on an economic system; not a critique of capitalism*. It is the emotions that these stories evoke that is primary, not so much the stories that evoke them. These emotions are the same, and the power of their critique derives from what they have in common.

What they had in common was not capitalism, but an image, a vision. It was a vision of being controlled by malevolent others, whose instrument is their control of the way we see things and, hence, how we live our lives. Both of these fictive worlds are built on the illusion that our ideas are our own products. But in fact, this vision goes on to say, those ideas are crafted for us so that we serve the purposes of those who create the ideas.

And yet, the visions continue, despite the resistance of the controllers, it is possible to see things as they really are. In that way, we can reclaim our real identities, from which we were lured away by the illusions, and re-establish an authentic life. This authentic life will not offer much comfort or amenity, and will even be dangerous, but it will be our own and will have a higher morality embedded in it: the morality of freedom and self-determination, and the possibility of a collective morality in the political struggle to free our fellow humans from their enslavement.

So how does capitalism fit into this? Capitalism, evidently, is just the symbolic framework; the metaphor, so to speak, through which we conceive of the underlying reality of oppression. It is the conscious content through which we try to comprehend something that is inherently unconscious. It could be done without entirely, while losing nothing that was essential.

And of course, if the Occupiers theory of capitalism is only an inadequate way of comprehending an underlying reality, the same may be said of the idea of being under the control of machines that have been spawned by a runaway Artificial Intelligence. It's just that we would never take such an idea literally.

But if the Thing and the Matrix are merely inadequate representations of an underlying reality, what is the underlying reality? This is, of course, a question that we cannot answer directly, but what we may be able to do is to shed some light on it by comprehending how it came about that we have it, and in that sense what it means.

Before we do that, however, I want to compare the Thing and the Matrix with a third system of illusion that does not arouse the same opposition. This is the system that Plato imagines in his allegory of the Cave.

Scenario Three: Plato's Cave

In *The Republic*, Plato (c. 380 BC) asks us to consider a world in which the people live their lives in a cave, chained to a wall, facing forward, and unable to change the direction of their gaze. Behind them, others pass back in forth in front of a fire that casts their shadows on a wall in front of the enchained people. The result is that they see nothing but shadows, and, since they see nothing else, they believe that the shadows constitute reality.

Now, one of the people is freed from his chains, so that he can see and move where he wants. At first, he sees the fire and the figures around him, but he thinks that these are illusions and that the shadows to which he has been accustomed are reality. But he is forced out of the cave where gradually he comes to see the world and finally the sun, and he comes to understand that the world of visible objects in the world outside the cave is reality. Pitying the people he has left behind, he goes back into the cave, where he becomes, no doubt, like whoever it was that first brought him to the light, and tries to convince the cave dwellers that they are living in illusion and should come into the light and see reality. But the people in the cave are committed to the idea that the shadows are reality. They note that he cannot see the illusions anymore and think him a fool. They say that going out of the cave evidently makes someone a fool and that they will kill anyone who tries to follow.

He really doesn't like the chore of bringing enlightenment, but he feels it is his obligation, so he makes it his work. He becomes a philosopher.

So here we see the same idea of the symbolic world as a system of illusion from which one can escape and see things as they really are. So far, the parallel with the Matrix and the Thing is perfect. But there is one thing that is missing, and that is the idea that all of this was created as expression of evil intent.

Plato does not at all consider the question of who chained the people to the wall in the first place, nor does he say anything about their moral character or their intent. And he does not suggest that the returning philosopher will be resisted by these chainers. Yet he wrote the story in order to make a point. If that had been the point, it would have been part of the story. If he had meant to say so, he would have said so. It isn't as if, if that were his point, he could have forgotten it.

Now, Plato understands, and says, that news of reality would be felt as a threat by those who live within the illusion, and that there would be an antagonism between the system and the philosopher who escapes and sees reality. But this antagonism is explained entirely by the anxiety of those within the system, who are ignorant, not evil. We simply do not see in Plato the idea that the world of illusion is the product of evil.

I think the conclusion we must draw from this is that the idea that we live in a world of illusion, and the idea that this is an expression of evil intent, that it is imposed by an evil force, are separate. One can have the first without the other.

What we need to do, therefore, is while staying with the premise of created illusion, to explain why this is seen in some cases as an assault, while in the other it is not.

The answer to this lies in the differentiation between Oedipal and anti-Oedipal psychologies that we have developed throughout this book, specifically pertaining to whether or not a person identifies with the father or not. This is presented below in terms of two more scenarios: Four and Five.

Scenario Four: The Classic Oedipus Complex

As we know, in Oedipal psychology, the child makes his peace with the father by idealizing him, internalizing him, and trying to become like him. The implicit promise is that father has earned mother's love. So if he becomes like father, he can earn mother's love as father has, thereby becoming again the center of a loving world.

This means taking into himself and making for his own the way the father defines himself and, hence, the way he understands the world, and justifies his life. These include the rules, norms, obligations, and common understandings that define the world and tell us how to operate within it.

In other words, it means identifying with the big Other, the symbolic order, culture, the common understandings, and beliefs that underlie society. The result of this is that, in place of being controlled by an outside force, he comes to be able to control himself so that he can direct his own life in accordance with the demands society makes and in the pursuit of his own desiderata. The image of doing so, of fusing again with the omnipotent and loving mother, as, in his fantasy, the father has, is called the ego ideal. Now he never gets to that point, never becomes the ego ideal, but through this process he gains a context, a set of narratives, in which he can locate his life, a sense of direction, a set of moral principles that will guide him in his pursuit of mother's love.

The point is that the idea of returning to being the center of a loving world is a fantasy; one can never attain it, but it is an important fantasy, since it gives meaning to work, organization, and whatever other institutions in society in which we participate in the attainment of socially approved goals. In other words, it is the psychological basis of society.

If we manage this successfully, our life has hope, which is the belief that the ego ideal can be obtained. That's as good as it gets.

But notice that the classic psychoanalytic account of socialization takes a similar view of the nature of social reality as we find in Plato. As I have said, psychoanalysis sees us spending our lives in pursuit of the ego ideal, which is a fantasy of being again one with mother. The pursuit of the ego ideal is a matter of "becoming like father," which means acting within the social reality, the big Other, in Lacan's terms, that the father represented and transmitted. But acting in accordance with our social reality always envisions a goal, under which, deeply or shallowly, lies the ego ideal.

But we never get to the ego ideal, and *this means that the structure of social reality, culture, the symbolic order, or whatever you like, which had the attainment of the ego ideal as the premise of all the behavior it defined and promoted, is a framework of illusion, in just the same way that the Thing, the Matrix, and the Cave are frameworks of illusion*. The difference is that, as in Plato, this framework is not seen as the product of malignant forces.

In a word, socialization means the induction into a world of illusion. Our question becomes how do we account for the experience of this illusion as an expression of a hostile force in the Thing and the Matrix, while it is a benign one in the Cave and in Oedipal psychology?

Scenario Five: The Anti-Oedipal

As we know, the transition into sociality that is portrayed in the Oedipal case depends on the premise of a good relationship between mother and father.

But we have seen that if mother identifies with the image of herself that the infant possesses: of omnipotence and benevolence, then, compared to what she could accomplish, the father's achievements would be like nothing. The boundary he created around her and the family would seem to be a trap. Its purpose would not be to keep harsh reality out, but to limit and control the expression of her love.

Under those circumstances, the child's idea that he will gain mother's love by becoming like the father is undermined. The father does not really possess mother's love, but only her body and her various services. If he has her love only on the basis of false pretenses, that means she does not really love him, the person he really is, at all. In that case, the rules, common understandings, obligations, that provided the context for mother's love for father come to be seen as the structures of that subterfuge, having the purpose of getting him what he wants, depriving the rest of us. Following the rules will make you guilty of the same crimes, and therefore as hateful as he is. You may gain the signs of love, such as money, prestige, and so on, but you will not gain its substance; your life will be empty.

Given this, it would seem that the route to closeness with the mother is not, as it was with the idealized father, through socially approved activity. On the contrary, activity in conformance with the social rules, such as work, for example, has been stripped of its connection with the ego ideal. To be sure, it never was connected to the ego ideal in reality, since the ego ideal is not in reality, but what kept society going was *the idea that* it was connected. It is that idea that has been rejected.

Rather, the idea is to join her in her disdain for the father. Taking that as our guide, our purpose will be to expel him from his place within the family. Then, mother's love will return to its proper object, which is us. In doing this, it is necessary to keep our vision clear and our motives pure. We must reclaim what remains of ourselves before socialization took us away for the dead end journey of following the father, or we must return to that state. This is our authentic self, and it is the proper object of mother's love.

Within this anti-Oedipal psychology, socialization comes to be seen as induction into a criminal enterprise. The rules and common understandings are not seen as ways for the individual to satisfy his real desires, but means by which the malevolent father validates himself, and traps those individuals into becoming as warped as he is.

What it produces cannot help but be corrupt and destructive. And the more it builds itself, the more powerful it becomes, and therefore the more destructive, and indeed the more inescapable. Following it means destroying and betraying ourselves.

The answer to this among those who joined Occupy was to say "Enough! I'll have none of this. I eschew the sense of direction that socialization, the father's stories, puts before me. I'll build my life around getting rid of the malevolent father; undermining and destroying his corrupt and destructive works. Instead of validating the views within which he defines his goodness, I'll show that these are self-serving fictions, masking his evil with a display of goodness. Instead of strengthening his world with my acquiescence and participation, I'll weaken it and ultimately bring it down. This is the way I will prove my worth and establish my claim to mother's love."

The Crux of the Matter

We see the social implications of this more clearly if we consider the father, not so much as an individual within a family, but in terms of what he is supposed to do, the *paternal function*; the function of creating and stabilizing a common framework of meaning, of structuring our way of seeing the world, and our place within it. This has been implicit in our discussion of the Oedipus complex, in the fact that socialization is always socialization into something specific.

The father, operating in fulfillment of the paternal function establishes that *this* is what you are supposed to do as a member of the society, and that *that*, which is to say action in violation of the rules and norms is something you are *not* supposed to do. In Lacan's words, the father's function, *le nom(n) du père*, is to establish law.

As I have said, the core of the paternal function is objective self-consciousness, which means learning to see yourself as an object, the way others would see you who are not connected with you. In other words, we, as well as all the other members learn a framework of meaning, for understanding people, that is common to all members of the society.

This is what makes it possible for us to predict the behavior of others, just as they predict ours, and therefore to coordinate our behavior with others in the pursuit of, not only our common, but our individual goals.

But we need to recall that the premise here is that, we adopt a view of ourselves within which, as members of the society, and subjects of the law, we are just like everybody else, and subject to the same rules.

We can see here the conflict with the way we are oriented toward the world under the aegis of the mother. She, and here I should recall that we are not talking about a real mother, but a very primitive conception of the mother, is the complement of our narcissism. But our narcissism is the pure negation of our commonality.

She loves us entirely, exactly as we are, and in the fullness of our uniqueness. Anything that we do will be perfect. We need not worry about running afoul of the world, because we are its center; the meaning of the world is to validate us. We are connected to the world, in Chasseguet-Smirgel's felicitous phrase, as if by an umbilical cord.

When we say that the mother hates the father, and that we join her in her disdain, what we are implicitly saying is that we have contempt for the social rules that tell us that we have to do things even if we don't want to do them. Instead, we choose a vision of the world in which we can do exactly what we want, without being subjected to constraint. Seeing ourselves as joining mother's disdain means that our safety will be guaranteed by the mother, the most powerful figure in the psyche.

This, at the deepest level, is what anti-Oedipal psychology, the repudiation of society, which is exactly that limiting frame of reference, comes down to. From this analysis, we can understand its appeal. It leaves us with the sense of being the center of a loving world that we began life with in the condition of primary narcissism. We are of cosmic significance, not because of what we have done, but simply because we are who we are. Who would give that up?

And who would not hate the father for trying to get us to give it up?

But what we need to see is that, without giving it up, we foreclose the possibility of society.

ALIENATION AT ZUCOTTI PARK

Anti-Oedipal psychology is against society; its *leitmotif* is alienation.

When I use the word "alienation," I use the term as it was used by Kenneth Keniston (1960) in a study of what he called "the uncommitted," a group of students at Harvard University. He defined the term as: "the rejection of the roles, values, and institutions [the alienated individual] sees as typical of adult American life" (p. 25). Keniston tells us that they had great contempt for those who blinded themselves to the realities of existence by buying into the traditional ways of seeing things in their society (p. 63). Of specific importance to us was their:

> fear and dislike of competition ... leading to an almost complete repudiation of the competitive business ethic of American society, to a dislike of and avoidance of social situations with a competitive quality, and to the continuing view that competition and rivalry, though ubiquitous, are destructive to all concerned. (p. 176)

What was interesting was that that this rejection was almost always accompanied by a more generalized alienated ideology, characterized by attitudes toward the self, to others, and to society in general, even going so far as to encompass attitudes toward the structure of the universe and the nature of knowledge. These students were solitary and lonely individualists, outsiders, living physically within society, but psychologically divorced from it (p. 73).

Looking into the family histories of these students, Keniston found a common pattern. The students were from middle-class families in which the father was seen as a loser. The mother, by contrast, was seen as strong and vital.

A typical family history went along with this. In this history, the parents began their marriage with high ideals, but lost their way. The father gave up his early ideals and settled into a career that would enable him to make as much money as possible. The mother gave up the ideal of a career that would permit the full expression of her talents and became a housewife.

As time went on, his career became the center of his life, which separated him physically and psychologically from his family. She thought less and less of him. For one thing, he did not, in her view, sufficiently support her in the realization of the visions she had for herself. Nor was he very much of a man. The focus of her emotional attachment became the son, rather than her husband. She shared her disappointment with her marriage and her husband, and assigned to the son the responsibility of fulfilling the ideals that were missing in her life.

The problem was that as she drew the son close to her emotionally, and made him responsible for her fulfillment, she simultaneously undercut the father who would ordinarily serve as the son's model of valued achievement. The result was that the son became what Keniston called a "pyrrhic victor in the Oedipal struggle." He was able to maintain the fantasy of a perfect fusion with his mother, but lost the possibility of forming the superego and integrating into the social order.

This would form a perfect fit for the anti-Oedipal model. Keniston characterizes them further:

> a central legacy of childhood for most of these alienated young men was the deep conviction that adult men—as epitomized by their own fathers—were not to be emulated, and the further belief that adulthood in general was disastrous insofar as it meant becoming like their fathers. (p. 178)
>
> The result is a diffusion and fragmentation of the sense of identity, an experience of themselves as amorphous, indistinct, and disorganized … Insofar as they have any clear sense of self it is almost entirely defined by what they are against, what they despise, by groups they do not want to belong to and values they consider tawdry. (p. 186)
>
> In [their] fantasies … we find [an] exaggerated dream of the blissfulness of early mother-son relationships, of the capacity of truly maternal women to provide totally for men, of the complete absence of distinctions between self and object. (p. 189)

In general, they lived, not with an eye to the future, but in the moment, placing their primary emphasis on experience and feeling, and on the cultivation of sentience and perceptiveness. Their goals and values were what he called "aesthetic," whose primary source is the self (p. 71). The primary drive is for passion and emotion, so reason must be subordinate to feeling. The obstacles are excessive self-control and social pressures that limit independence (p. 72). But all of social order limits independence, so the enemy here is the whole social order, the whole cultural ethos, not merely parts of it that could be changed to make it better.

What we see in the Occupy movement is the manifestation of this alienated outlook in the form of politics.

The worlds of created illusion seen in The Matrix and Communique #1 are society seen from the outside, the standpoint of alienation. The evil figure who created and controls this symbolic monstrosity, for the purpose of stealing mother's love, is the father. He and the system that expresses him, are the bad object. Its badness consists in depriving us of love.

In the Occupy case, that bad object is identified as Wall Street, which refers to the father and the father's system, capitalism, which expresses him and that seeks to extinguish us, causing us to lose our specific identities and become parts of the system. But the problem is not located in the specific qualities of the system. Any society is a pre-existing system that we have to fit into, and therefore poses constraints to our authentic and spontaneous expression, and to our sense of cosmic importance.

We can see this most clearly at the end of the Matrix, when Neo issues his threat to the machines. Recall what he says:

> I'm going to show these people what you don't want them to see. I'm going to show them a world without you … a world without rules and controls, without borders or boundaries. A world … where anything is possible.

But the world without rules and controls is the ego ideal, and that cannot be realized in any real society. To condemn anything that falls short of that is simple nihilism.

General Implications for Work, Organization, and Revolution

Our purpose in this chapter has been to figure out what the OWS protest is a protest against. We started with the premise that it was capitalism, but argued that this was not capitalism as an economic system, but as an element in a morality play; capitalism, as the expression of the father, is a bad object. But what has been said of capitalism here could have been said of any way of organizing society. They are all products of the paternal function.

I want to show the generalizability of this by discussing some fundamental features of society.

As we have seen, the paternal principle and objective self-consciousness create the structure of society. They create impersonal rules that apply to everyone and make us comprehensible to one another.

Gouldner (1960) tells us that the most fundamental of these are rules that govern exchange relationships, which derive from what he has called the *norm of reciprocity*: "You *should* give benefits to those who give you benefits."

From the norm of reciprocity derives the common framework of rules that we have called society. We may think of it as a set of interlinked hypothetical propositions of the form *If A does X, B should do Y*, where we can think of ourselves, indifferently, as being in either the A position or the B position. Within this set of rules, I can anticipate that if I, as A, do X, somebody else, as B, who I have reason to believe will also operate within this set of rules, will understand that they must reciprocate, which in this case means they must do Y.

We must understand how critical this is in the construction of any society, including any organization. They are the social conditions that make purposive social interaction possible. They give sense to the idea that I can do X for the purpose of getting Y.

If we wanted to derive a theory of society, or organization, from this, we could show how such exchanges would come under the control of rules of exchange. For instance we could draw the implication that such a person, as B, would be expected by all others who buy into this framework of rules, and who are dependent on their operation, to do Y. This would show how the enforcement of the provisions of a contract would be legitimized. And we could show the way these rules are internalized to form the superego, and how through the superego, we make external enforcement unnecessary by enforcing our obligations through our own sense of guilt.

Exchange operates through our infliction of guilt upon ourselves for violation of the norm of reciprocity. This is certainly one aspect of what Freud had in mind when he claimed, in *Civilization and its Discontents*, (1962) that the feeling of guilt is the psychological force that underlies civilization (Kultur). Nietzsche (1989) says basically the same thing when he points out the kinship between the German words for guilt (schuld) and debt (schulden) and he goes a bit further in maintaining that this is the basic mechanism of exchange, which is the root not only of all social order, but of thought, the symbolic order, and society itself.

A constitutive element of this is indebtedness, which refers to exchange relationships that have not been balanced yet by the reciprocation of benefits. For Gouldner, it is the emotional glue that holds otherwise distant members of the society together; indeed, it makes society possible.

This is true not only of developed societies, according to Gouldner, but to all of them. For this, he cites Malinowski's work on the Trobriand Islanders, where he notes that tribesmen perform their ritual activities with the belief in mind that, although there is no immediate payment, in the end it all balances out.

The manifest program of OWS is the destruction of capitalism. But capitalism is no more nor less that the structure of exchange relationships in contemporary society. It follows that the underlying program of OWS is the repudiation of the norm of reciprocity and the related concepts of indebtedness and guilt. This constitutes assault upon the very possibility of society.

Strike Debt: An Application

But it turns out to be very close to the center of the political program of OWS.

This takes the form of an offshoot called Strike Debt, whose views are expressed in an article in the third issue of *Tidal* (Folks 2012), and in their publication *The Debt Resistors Operations Manual* (DROM) (Anonymous, 2012) which is available at their website http://strikedebt.org.

The primary premise here is that "mafia capitalism," by which they mean the same thing as "capitalism" without the modifier, has forced just about everybody into debt as a way of exploiting and oppressing them.

> Everyone seems to owe something, and most of us (including our cities) are in so deep it'll be years before we have any chance of getting out—if we have any chance at all. At least one in seven of us is already being pursued by debt collectors. We are told all of this is our own fault, that we got ourselves into this and that we should feel guilty or ashamed. (DROM, p. 1)

The whole system in which we live and in which we participate is part of this apparatus:

> [I]t's a shakedown system. The financial establishment colludes with the government to create rules designed to put everyone in debt; then the system extracts it from you. ... it means endlessly making up new rules designed to put us all in debt, with the entire apparatus of government, police and prisons providing enforcement and surveillance. (DROM, p. 1)

This holds true as well for our individual behavior:

> Debt is immoral. It is indentured servitude, a type of bondage ... We have to sell our time, our souls, working jobs we don't care about simply so we can pay interest to the bank. Now that debt is so rampant, many of us are ashamed for putting others in debt. Our professions from teacher to lawyer and physician have become means to direct more victims to the loan sharks. (Folks, p. 10)

Society, they say, tells us we are obliged to pay back this debt, and should feel guilty and ashamed if we do not. But they refuse to feel that way:

> We are under no moral obligation to keep our promises to liars and thieves. In fact, we are morally obligated to find a way to stop this system rather than continuing to perpetuate it. (DROM, p. 2)

The OWS modality for doing this is what they call a debt strike, which they see as part of a revolutionary movement to destroy the system and reclaim their lives.

> When we strike debt, we live a life rather than repay a loan. We refuse to mortgage our lives. We reject the math that debt forces on us; math that says we cannot "afford" to care for our communities because we must "pay back" the banks forever, above and beyond what was borrowed. We question the dominance of the market in every aspect of social and cultural life. (Folks, p. 11)

And:

> Strike Debt seeks to abolish debt as it currently exists and reconstruct a just society where our debts and bonds are to one another and not the 1%. (Folks, p. 11)

So the 99 % are under no obligation to pay any of the debt. Refusing to do so is an act of righteousness, in which people chose freedom, living their lives, and giving to those who love them, and whom they love, instead of continuing to participate in the debt system.

From our point of view, it is clear enough what has happened here. Society's structure has been rejected; its meanings denied. What we do in balancing exchange relationships is a proxy for socialized activity as a whole, which is now looked at from the standpoint of alienation. The meanings that society has given to the constraints it imposes have been rejected and the imposition itself has become an act of paternal oppression.

Let us go back over their case:

The central move here is that the paternal function has been repudiated, and especially objective self-consciousness. It was objective self-consciousness, we recall, that made it possible for us to understand each other in objective terms. This was what made possible the kind of impersonal exchange that organization is made out of, which is to say organization that does not depend on specific emotional connections.

When they say that they "reject the math" that says we must pay back the banks instead of caring for our communities, what they mean is that they reject the rules that structure exchange among people who have no emotional connections with each other. They see these rules as expressing the domination of the 1 %, which is to say the father's domination. They chose to reconstruct a society in which all interaction is among people who are emotionally and specifically connected to each other. But as we recall from Chapter 3, in the absence of structure, even these collapse.

Work within the society, insofar as it is structured by these objective rules of exchange, is the imposition of the father's oppression. It is stripped of its connection to the ego ideal and cannot make sense, so it must be felt as an intolerable burden. It must be felt to be "indentured servitude, a type of bondage ... We have to sell our time, our souls, working jobs we don't care about simply so we can pay interest to the bank."

The connection to the ego ideal having been removed, the whole realm of socialized activity is redefined within the context of hopelessness, and therefore as negative.

There is no recognition that exchange works in both directions; that the person who borrows money actually gets something through the money that has been borrowed. Rather, exchange is defined as loss. But since there is no benefit gained from exchange, there cannot be any reason for incurring debt, and therefore no such thing as debt freely entered into. We are in debt because we have been caused by to be so by the system's malevolence. We have been deceived into believing we want or need things that the system has created for the purpose of entrapping us, and then we are kept in the system by force. All lending, that is to say, is predatory lending.

The failure to differentiate applies in the other direction as well. Everything we have that is good, they believe, was freely given to us by those who love us. This is the way it would be for everybody, if the world were in proper moral order. They make the assumption that, through love, everything good would be freely given to everyone in our communities, all of whose members are connected by love. This would have obviated the need to enter into the debt system all together.

Rejecting the father means that we do not need to submit to our diminution by entering into this system wherein we are just like everyone else. On the contrary, our singular importance can be preserved, together with the possibility of relating only to others with whom we are emotionally connected; indeed, with whom we identify, and whose own grandeur is in that way assured. All we need to do is get rid of the father and his works. Maternal love will provide.

But, of course, it will not.

Social Control in the Occupy Movement

The repudiation of objective self-consciousness means losing the possibility of organizing ourselves through self-control and the self-imposition of social order. Interestingly one could see this play out in the deterioration of the social system that structured, and then failed to structure, OWS.

An excellent journalistic record of this was provided by Quinn Norton in *Wired Magazine* (2012) under the title "A Eulogy for #Occupy." Norton, an astute and sympathetic participant observer who saw herself as being "in but not of" Occupy, covered the movement's development, beginning three weeks after its inauguration until its demise. Her story centers around the rise and fall of Occupy's self-governing system, the GA. This was an idea adopted from the *Indignados*, a group that arose in Spain in opposition to the austerity measures imposed by the EU.

The GA was based on a principle of radical inclusion, and of bringing everyone's voice into everything the group did, ideally driving toward consensus on everything. The stylistic novelties that came to be associated with Occupy's ways of doing things, such as the twinkling hand gestures and the "people's mike," in which the group repeated in unison what speakers said, were part of the GA's process. It had not only a legislative function, but executive and judicial ones as well. They organized their cooking and eating processes on this model and solved small disputes as well. It was not only Occupy's means of organization, it was supposed to serve as a model of what organization would look like in the happy future that Occupy wanted to bring about. As Norton put it: "At first, like so many parts of Occupy, it was a wonder to see."

But over time, the GA came under the domination of the sort of forces to which anarchy is always vulnerable. By including everything, the GA gave up any way of defending itself against the self-destructive impulses that it had made part of itself.

> By the time I returned to NY … the NYC GA was a place where women were threatened with beatings, and street kids with calls to the police. All

> the reasonable people had gotten the fuck out. It had become a gladiator pit no one enjoyed watching. Even Weev, the famous internet troll, didn't last through the nastiness of the GA I took him to. He left while I wasn't looking, without saying goodbye. We never spoke about it. I didn't blame him, and I didn't have to ask why. It was the tiny, brutal, and bitter politics of failed people.
>
> Because the GA had no way to reject force, over time it fell to force. Proposals won by intimidation; bullies carried the day. What began as a way to let people reform and remake themselves had no mechanism for dealing with them when they didn't. It had no way to deal with parasites and predators. It became a diseased process, pushing out the weak and quiet it had meant to enfranchise until it finally collapsed when nothing was left but predators trying to rip out each other's throats

And it had no way of correcting its processes by learning from its errors:

> There was no critique in Occupy, no accountability. At first it didn't matter, but as life grew messy and complicated, its absence became terrible. There wasn't even a way to conceive of critique, as if the language had no words to describe the movement's faults to itself. ... Self-censorship plagued those who weren't gagged, because everyone was afraid of retaliation. No one talked about the systemic and growing abuses in the camps, or the increasingly poisonous GAs.

As a result:

> The idea of the GA—its process, its form, inclusiveness—failed. It had all the best chances to evolve, imprinted on the consciousness of thousands of occupiers like a second language. No idea gets a better chance than that, and it still failed.

What was lacking was objective self-consciousness, which was therefore unavailable for them to apply to themselves: "*There wasn't even a way to conceive of critique, as if the language had no words to describe the movement's faults to itself,*" to repeat her words.

My claim is that this conjoint failure was inevitable. It was built into the core of the system; it was what Occupy was all about: the assault against the father and the paternal function.

The Overwhelming Question: How Shall We See Society?

We need to take account of these two different views of the nature of socialization, remarkably similar but strikingly different, based on the orientation taken toward the father, and whether or not he is identified with, or experienced as evil.

With identification, and without the coloration of evil, society is not only not the product of malignant forces, but is an actual beneficence, one might even say a blessing. It is the framework that gives us a sense of direction in our lives, it gives us a setting in which our lives can make sense to us. Indeed, in a very literal way, it is the sense that our lives have, insofar as we make sense of them. In other words, it is sense itself. If our lives have meaning, this is the meaning they have. We may take this meaning passively, or actively make it our own through existential choice, but it is all that there is. Moreover, it gives us the only hope that humans can have. Hope is a belief that it is possible to attain the ego ideal. It is only within society that the ego ideal can be specified and means of attainment can be conceived. And it is only as means of attainment of the ego ideal that anything we do can have sense.

But all of this is lost to the person who refuses society. Its virtues are only seen from the standpoint of someone who sees it from within.

And here is the Achilles heel, not only of this society, but also of any society. The existential truth is that we are all marginal.

What OWS has seen is that a society is based on myths, and these myths cannot prove their truth because they are not true. What would be the premises from which we could demonstrate their validity? They would have to arise from another social system, which would have exactly the same problems of unprovability. The great Ernest Becker (1974) called them vital lies. We need to believe them if our lives are to make sense, but we cannot give them any substantive base.

In the absence of that, it makes perfectly good sense to suppose that society is a system of falsehood which is being imposed on us by those who want to deprive us of the only thing that is really our own, which is ourselves. Thinking about our lives in this way, society is seen, in its basic constitution, as a threat to our lives. It is not surprising that this would be seen as essentially evil; as the bad object.

The only sense our lives could have in such a circumstance would be by relating to society as its negation. In the name of honesty, or authenticity, or truth, we could make sense of our lives by being against society, seeing it as an alien imposition.

Seen in this way, resistance to it, and even the destruction of it, make perfectly good sense. They are, indeed, the only framework of meaning that is available to us. But they preserve something, which is our own authentic self.

This is, of course the view from Zucotti Park.

But look how barren it is. Their idea of what they are doing authorizes and gives sense only to the destruction of the father and his works. The idea of the authentic self they celebrate is a minimal self. Take away the direction provided by the negation of the father and this is a self entirely without dimensions, living a life without any parameters. They can associate with others, but such association offers nothing but association itself, and with other people as minimal as themselves, indeed identical in their minimality.

Their problem goes right back to their origin, and it is that their whole purpose is to return to their origin. Goodness was in the past, they think, and therefore it makes no sense to connect themselves to anything in the future. But that rules out the entire category of *becoming*. The self that remains is a zero and likely to remain so. Whatever potential such a being may have can be realized only through inadvertence.

It's worse even than that. Their opposition to society, ironically, is rooted just as much in a system of falsehood as the society they oppose. The fantasy here is that if we kill father, we can marry mother. But, in reality, we will not marry mother whether we kill father or not. And even if we did, we would find that it isn't all we imagined it would be. Remember that the appeal of fusing again with mother, forming a boundaryless connection, is based on the premise that we can return to that infantile condition, and any comprehension of reality will assure us that we cannot.

Finally, it may be interesting to return to our beginning. We saw that the critique of OWS made much of the idea that they have not made any demands. We saw that the truth of this is that they have had nothing to offer in the way of an alternative conception of the way society could function. We can now see that this is a consequence of their most basic premise. The attack upon the father is at the same time an attack upon objective self-consciousness and the idea of social structure. But any alternative conception of the way society could function would be an idea of social structure. They are not providing an alternative idea of the way society could function, not because they are not smart, or lack imagination, or haven't thought about the matter in the right way; it follows from the very core of what they are doing.

An Overview

This brings us to a point where we can place this critique into perspective. I may have given the impression that I think of the Occupy movement as some kind of threat to social order. I do not. As a movement, it never amounted to much and has largely faded away, the way such "revolutionary" movements have always faded away in America.

What is important about it is the light it sheds on the fragility of our society.

We can see this in the muteness of the response; the fact that the society could not bring itself to defend itself. The charges leveled by OWS were stereotypic and sophomoric; they should have been easy to respond to, but responses were not forthcoming. Why was that?

We know that it had to do with the unprovability of the myths and beliefs at the root of society. But these myths have always been unprovable. Why has that become a problem now?

St Augustine (419) said "Understanding is the reward of faith. Therefore, seek not to understand that you may believe, but believe that you may understand."

This reminds us that the grounding of society has always taken place within the dominion of faith. That suggests that the problems to which OWS calls attention concern not so much the failure of capitalism, but the decline of traditional religion.

A friend once told me that the conception of society I have developed provided an excellent picture of the world without God.

Maybe so.

But there can be religion without God. And the practice of that religion at Zucotti Park, as at Oberlin and elsewhere, is what we have here.

Notes

1. Anne Applebaum (2012) has published a marvelous study of the failure of the communist system in Eastern Europe, following its imposition, on vulnerable societies, under Soviet guidance, following World War II.
2. Note that for an organization like this, which sees itself as having a collective identity, an authoritative statement is more likely to be unsigned than

signed, since it could not be taken to be the view of a single person. This, of course, creates the possibility of somebody knocking off just any old thing, and having it taken as authoritative. This is an instance of a more general problem, which we will engage later.

3. The success of The Matrix led to the production of two sequels, released in 2003, as well as video games and comic books. For the purposes of this analysis, the first movie will be considered by itself.

References

Anonymous. 2011. Communiqué #1. *Tidal: Occupy Theory, Occupy Strategy.* December, Issue 1. http://tidalmag.org/pdf/tidal1_the-beginning-is-near.pdf

———. 2012. The Debt Resistors Operations Manual (DROM). http://strikedebt.org.

Applebaum, Anne. 2012. *Iron Curtain: The Crushing of Eastern Europe: 1944–1956.* New York: Doubleday.

Becker, Ernest. 1974. *The Denial of Death.* New York: The Free Press.

Butler, Judith. 2011. For and Against Precarity. *Tidal: Occupy Theory, Occupy Strategy*, December, Issue 1. http://tidalmag.org/pdf/tidal1_the-beginning-is-near.pdf.

Folks from Strike Debt. 2012. Strike Debt. *Tidal: Occupy Theory, Occupy Strategy*, September.

Freud, Sigmund. 1962. *Civilization and its Discontents.* First American edition. Trans. and ed. James Strachey. New York: Norton.

Gouldner, Alvin W. 1960. The Norm of Reciprocity: A Preliminary Statement. *American Sociological Review* 25: 161–178.

Hardt, Michael, and Antonio Negri. 2012. Declaration. Allen, Texas: Argo Navis.

Keniston, Kenneth. 1960. *The Uncommitted: Alienated Youth in American Society.* New York: Harcourt.

Nietzsche, Friedrich. 1989. *On the Genealogy of Morals: A Polemical Tract.* On the Genealogy of Morals and Ecce Homo (Reissue Edition) translated by Walter Kaufman. New York: Vintage.

Norton, Quinn. 2012. A Eulogy for #Occupied. *Wired Magazine*, December 12. http://www.wired.com/2012/12/a-eulogy-for-occupy/all/.

Plato. c. 380 BC. *The Republic.*

St. Augustine. 419. Tractates on the Gospel of John. Tractate 29.

Wachowski, Larry, and Andy Wachowski. 1999. *The Matrix.* Los Angeles: Warner Brothers. http://www.screenplay.com/downloads/scripts/The%20Matrix.pdf.

Žižek, Slavoj. 2011. Occupy First. Demands Come Later. *The Guardian,* October 26.

Žižek, Slavoj. 2012. *The Year of Dreaming Dangerously.* London: Verso.

CHAPTER 8

Conclusion: Christakis at Thermopylae

In the end it is good to go back to the beginning.

We began with an introduction in which I invoked an outrage of the day, which was the assault on the spirit of Halloween for committing the sin of the day, which was "cultural appropriation." I said at the time that I would stick to that outrage, just to get the book done, despite my expectation that the next day would bring a new outrage begging to be incorporated and chronicled, which would be followed by a new one on the day after that, and so on. I was certainly right to cut that short.

In fact, the attack upon Halloween gave birth to a slew of absurdities, each one more weird than the one before, culminating in an event at Yale University that instantly became a classic. The associated drama manifested some of the dynamics we have discussed. I'll go through it and bring these out.

The origin of this particular tempest was an email message sent out on 27 October to the Yale student body by the university's Intercultural Affairs Committee (IAC), and signed by 13 diversity officials (2015). It said, in part, that Halloween is a time when the normal sensitivity and thoughtfulness of Yale students can be forgotten, and in which choices of costume can be made that offend or denigrate members of various cultural groups. They offered feathered headdresses and turbans as examples. Therefore, while students definitely had the right to express themselves, it was hoped that they would "actively avoid those circumstances that

H.S. Schwartz, *Political Correctness and the Destruction of Social Order*, DOI 10.1007/978-3-319-39805-1_8

threaten our sense of community or disrespects, alienates or ridicules segments of our population based on race, nationality, religious belief or gender expression." Even choices made with no intention to offend they said, "have sent a far greater message than any apology could after the fact."

And so they recommended that before students put on a costume, they should take the time to consider what impact their choices might have by asking themselves questions like these:

- Wearing a funny costume? Is the humor based on "making fun" of real people, human traits, or cultures?
- Wearing a historical costume? If this costume is meant to be historical, does it further misinformation or historical and cultural inaccuracies?
- Wearing a "cultural" costume? Does this costume reduce cultural differences to jokes or stereotypes?
- Could someone take offense with your costume and why?

At the first instance, it is clear enough that program represents Rule Two of political correctness that we discussed regarding the Oberlin case: Love the oppressed, whom it lists. But it also brings in Rule One, which is hate the father, which means everyone else, and specifically the usual suspects: white, heterosexual males, and whoever would take the side of these others in an argument. But it is more interesting, perhaps, to see it as an expression of the Rule Three, which is to keep the political correctness drama going. As I pointed out above, the issues raised in these dramas are never the issues, except as pretexts for holding the dramas. It is impossible to believe that this program was developed as a response to real pain. As Erika Christakis put it in the next act of the drama, "no one around campus seems overly concerned about the offense taken by religiously conservative folks to skin-revealing costumes," I suggest, rather, that nobody was ever in any real doubt that Halloween was Halloween, except until the IAC wanted to use it to make a point. Their aim here was to display their power, and power is never really seen until it encounters opposition. It is only then that the drama of political correctness comes alive. It would go too far to say that this group of bureaucrats consciously made this an issue for the sake of picking a fight, but at some level they knew that it would serve their purpose if they got one.

At any rate, if they were looking for opposition, they got it in the person of Ms. Christakis, a professor of childhood development and Associate

Master of Silliman Residential College, who on 30 October urged a bit of lightening up (2015). Mobilizing perhaps the only type of argument that she thought could have some appeal, she pointed to the transgressive quality of the holiday. Halloween, she said, has always been a time for children to subvert the established order. Yet it has also been a time for adults to exert their control, and that is what she saw in the IAC message. And she said it was a problem:

> Pretend play is the foundation of most cognitive tasks, and it seems to me that we want to be in the business of encouraging the exercise of imagination, not constraining it. I suppose we could agree that there is a difference between fantasizing about an individual character vs. appropriating a culture, wholesale, the latter of which could be seen as (tacky) (offensive) (jejeune) (hurtful), take your pick. But, then, I wonder what is the statute of limitations on dreaming of dressing as Tiana the Frog Princess if you aren't a black girl from New Orleans?
>
> Is there no room anymore for a child or young person to be a little bit obnoxious … a little bit inappropriate or provocative or, yes, offensive? American universities were once a safe space not only for maturation but also for a certain regressive, or even transgressive, experience; increasingly, it seems, they have become places of censure and prohibition. And the censure and prohibition come from above, not from yourselves! Are we all okay with this transfer of power?

And she quotes her husband, a professor of sociology and Master of Silliman, saying:

> Nicholas says, if you don't like a costume someone is wearing, look away, or tell them you are offended. Talk to each other. Free speech and the ability to tolerate offence are the hallmarks of a free and open society

Well, evidently there is no such room, or even any room for raising the question. The purpose of political correctness, after all, is to brook no criticism of itself. The whole university took the occasion to be outraged by Christakis's message. Many called for her resignation and that of her husband. A group called Concerned Yale Students, Alumni, Family, Faculty, and Staff (2015) wrote an open letter, which gathered more than a thousand signatures, mostly from undergraduates, that laid out the terms of their indictment. It said, among other things, that to compare a suggestion made by the IAC, which was created to challenge bias, to an exercise of institutional control erases the voices of those the committee was set up to protect. And that comparing the use of harmful stereotypes that degrade marginalized people to preschoolers playing make believe trivializes the harm that is done. "In your email, you ask students to 'look away' if costumes are offensive, as if the degradation of our cultures and people, and the violence that grows out of it is something that we can ignore." And so on.

Dissecting its logic in *The Atlantic*, Conor Friedersdorf (2015) pointed out that it doesn't make any sense. It doesn't have to; it employs Rule Four: invoke the love and power of mother.

But the most striking manifestation of this collective frenzy was on 5 November, when a group of about 100 students gathered around Nicholas Christakis and demanded an apology for Erika's email. I will turn now to an analysis of that encounter.

Nicholas and the Barbarians

For the purposes of this analysis, I will rely upon three videos of this event, which have been posted at YouTube under the titles Yale University Students Protest Halloween Costume Email (VIDEO 1) (VIDEO 2) (VIDEO 3) by the Foundation for Individual Rights in Education (FIRE). FIRE has also posted transcripts of Videos 2 and 3. All of this material is available through FIRE (2015).

There do not seem to be any videos that encompass the whole crowd, but Inspection of the videos at YouTube suggests that those in the first line of the confrontation are about half black, with the remainder being about equally white and Asian. Speakers A, B, and C, as denominated by FIRE, are black women.

I want to offer a close analysis of this series of transactions, and for that purpose transcriptions will be necessary. At various places in the transcripts, the term "(snaps)" is employed. This refers to students snapping their fingers, which is evidently a form of applause. I will use the FIRE transcriptions for Videos 2 and 3. There is no posted transcript for Video 1, probably because much of it is inaudible. My best estimate is this:

Student A: (inaudible) I live here. I eat in the dining halls for all three meals, and you should know my name. My name is Michaela, but people have called me other names. People have called me

Jeralynn, people have called me Malika, people have called me Nina

Christakis: Now, I've learned Jeralynn, and I've learned Malika, and I've learned …

Crowd: Applause.

Christakis: (Raises his arms to accept applause) Thank you. (inaudible) 500 names. I have 500 names to learn, (inaudible) I have 500 names to learn. And if you'd like to see the personal effects my difficulty in learning names, you can.

Student A: I do see it. Okay. But I have a point, because …

Christakis: But Michaela, you have to understand it has nothing to do with your race, my difficulty learning names, inaudible

Student A: Well, but that's how it seems, because I have been here …

It will escape no one's notice that he has denied that his evident incapacity to remember her name was due to her race, whatever that may mean. And she says that it seemed that way, whatever that could mean. But, indeed, what *could* it mean? Her point, here, seems to be that since she has been here so long, he should know her name, and if he does not, it must be because of her race. But she does not base this claim on an observed connection between his behavior and anything in his mind. Her move is one that the Macpherson Commission would have seen as an inference, and they would have regarded it as valid. But, as in their case, we can see that it is not an inference at all. In the absence of anything else, it is a logical *non sequitur*.

Yet leaving it at that would miss the dynamics that are in operation here; the grounding of her claim is psychological, not logical. She is taking herself as the pristine self. As we saw above in the analysis of microaggression, he is required to take her as unique, in the way that she takes herself to be unique. Her race is the basis on which she asserts her claim. For her, that is a necessary and sufficient condition for an accusation of racism. Christakis continues:

Christakis: I know but can you see, can you see, for example, can you play music?

Student A: Okay.

Christakis: I cannot play music, so when people try to talk to me about musical things, I don't understand.

Crowd: (inaudible) How is this …

Christakis: (addressing the crowd, evidently trying to explain the form of his reasoning) I'm making an idea. I'm expressing that one of my limitations as a person, which I always had was I wasn't very good at memorizing names, and it's got nothing to do with race, Michaela. I think this conversation in its intensity, will really seal it. And I hope, in my primary interaction with you, I've never treated you with any disrespect.
Student A: And you haven't. I was about to say, in the class that I took this Fall …

Video 2 continues with Student A, but at a somewhat later point. The focus has become Erika's email:

Student A: I give tours every day—not if every week—and have to stand here in the courtyard and say "This is my home. I live up there. My master's there; my dean. I love my college." And I can't say that anymore because it's not a home. It is no longer a safe space for me.

And she demands an apology.

> in your role as master and associate master, after sending that email and after not having an appropriate response, that our opinion has been dismissed. That you guys have not said "I hear you. I hear that you are hurting and I am sorry that I have caused you to feel pain." I have not heard that from you and I have not heard that from your wife. And that is what I want to hear. I don't want to hear anymore [inaudible] because it's not fair [inaudible].

The opening of Christakis' response is inaudible. Someone in the crowd says "speak up." Then we hear him say:

Christakis: I don't want to look away from her …
Student in crowd: Just talk louder and look at her!

Whereupon, with passion, he reveals to them the difficulty of his position. He cannot speak loudly enough for everyone to hear while continuing to look in her direction, since then he will appear to be yelling at her:

Christakis: (loudly, he is clearly frustrated) I'm doing my best, everyone. I'm doing my best. I'm doing my best. I'm trying to address her directly and as a human being, face to face, and I don't want to turn my back to her. And I don't want to yell at her, I'm this far, if I raise my voice so you can hear me.

Student in crowd: Thank you.

Christakis: So please stop misjudging anything I do, ok. Give me a little bit of talking room, alright? So as I was telling you … I'll speak up a little, but I won't yell at her. That fair?

And they give him a break:

Student in crowd: Yes.

Student in crowd: That's fair.

Now, it is the speech of Student C, to which we will turn below, that has given this interaction its notoriety, but I submit that this interchange between Christakis and the students is crucial to understanding what is going on. Christakis is fearful that what he is saying will be subject to misinterpretation; that he will be seen in ways that do not properly take account of his thoughts or feelings. He believes that he must anticipate these possible misinterpretations and preclude their application; if he gets it wrong, it will be interpreted as racism. But he is finding it impossible, in these circumstances, to get it right. In this environment, for example, to speak loudly while looking at Student A may seem to some to be reminiscent of the way that masters abused their slaves. On the other hand, to look away and speak loudly, so that the rest of the crowd can hear him, puts him in danger of seeming to dismiss Student A, silencing her voice, and so on, the way that white people have always dismissed black people and their concerns.

Christakis is doing the dance of political correctness, but the choreography is breaking down. There is no clearly defined safe move that he can make. So he metacommunicates. He talks about the difficulty of his position. And the students buy his explanation. *But that has to mean that they understand the dance of political correctness to be a dance.* They know that Christakis harbors no racist thoughts or feelings, and the danger that he faces is not that of being misinterpreted as such. What they are calling upon him to do has nothing to do with racism, except insofar as it is a gambit that can be played in a game whose meaning is domination. They are calling upon him to recognize who is boss. He is doing his best to retain some of his dignity, but by asking them for permission to speak, he acknowledges that they are running the show. Here again we have Rule Three.

At any rate, having been granted that permission. He continues speaking to Student A, Michaela, who has been in class with him, expressing amazement that she has not been able to form an opinion of him as a person and to see the extent to which he agrees with the content of her beliefs. She is not mollified. She says "I don't see you as agreeing," but it appears that the pursuit of this dialogue has exhausted the patience of some in the audience, who want to cut to the core of the issue. He needs to just submit and shut up.

Student B: Can I, can I say something? Can I, can I just interject really quickly? The moral of Michaela's comments is not … The moral of the story is, she wants an apology, yet you respond not with an apology. … Are you going to address the heart of her comment? That's all I want. Are you gonna give an apology? Are you gonna say that you're hearing us? Are you gonna, then, go to the lengths that she wants you to go to which, to me, don't seem very far. But, still seem … We're not making a judgment on like, Master Christakis is inherently b—like, we just want an acknowledgement of hurt, and we have yet to get that which Michaela just said.

Crowd: [Snaps.]

Student B: So, my question is: are you going to say that? Or not? Cause then, I could just leave if you're not gonna say that. Cause, I've heard from … I was at the discussion, I was here, I'm gonna be there on Sunday, and I'm gonna listen. But, like, what I'm listening for, I've not yet heard. So I'm just asking, are you gonna provide that or are you not gonna provide that.

He then goes through a Socratic routine, whose aim is to get them to see the complexities that would arise from his offering an apology in this case, but it again appears that he has lost the patience of his audience, because now comes the high point of the afternoon, if not the decade:

Christakis: [Possibly to Student B] Other people have rights, too! Not just you.

Student in crowd:	Walk away. Walk away. [inaudible] He doesn't deserve to be listened to.
Crowd:	[Jeers.]
Student C:	[Inaudible] create an unsafe space here for all [inaudible]
Christakis:	I do not …
Student C:	Be quiet! …

The rage in this student's voice is jarring. He visibly recoils from it but immediately returns to his posture of humility. His hands are folded in front of his chest, in a gesture we associate with a supplicant. She continues:

Student C:	For all Silliman students. Do you understand that? As your position as master, it is your job to create a place of comfort and home for the students that live in Silliman.
Christakis:	I hear you.
Student C:	You have not done that. By sending out that email, that goes against your position as master. Do you understand that?
Christakis:	No I don't agree with that.
Student C:	[Yelling.] Then why the fuck did you accept the position!
Christakis:	Because I have a diff …
Student C:	[Yelling.] Who the fuck hired you?
Christakis:	I have a different vision than you.
Student C:	[Yelling.] Then step down! If that is what you think about being a [inaudible] master, then you should step down. It is not about creating an intellectual space! It is not! Do you understand that? It's about creating a home here! You are not doing that. You're going against that.
Student in crowd:	You're supposed to be our advocate!
Student C:	You should [inaudible] be at the event last night when you hear [inaudible] say that she didn't know how to create a safe space for her freshman at Silliman! How do you explain that? Because freshman come here and they think this is what Yale is? You hear that?

	They're gonna leave! They're gonna transfer because you are a poor steward of the community.
Student in crowd:	Retweet!
Student C:	You should not sleep at night!
Students in crowd:	We out. We out.
Student C:	You are disgusting.

I want to take a look at this remarkable ejaculation in the light of what we have seen. To begin with, consider her claim that

> as master, it is your job to create a place of comfort and home for the students that live in Silliman. … It is not about creating an intellectual space! It is not! Do you understand that? It's about creating a home here! You are not doing that. You're going against that.

This is as clear an invocation of the pristine self as we are likely to hear. And her clear belief that she, an undergraduate, has the authority to tell this man, the master of her residential college, a distinguished professor of sociology, and a physician, what his job is, and to express her utter contempt for his thoughts about the matter, together with his near submissiveness in the face of it, says as much about the normalization of the pristine self as one is likely to encounter.

But what grabs the attention here is the sheer rage of Student C and particularly the clear absence of any attempt to moderate it. What we see here is the pure hatred of the father, in a situation where that hatred is reinforced and validated. It is the tone that a superior takes toward an inferior, in which the superior has no fear of retaliation.

This is the voice of the primordial mother. It is powerful stuff, and who will stand in its way?

We need to consider what is at issue here. Students A, B, and C tell us that they feel unsafe, threatened. And the whole rageful protest that began with the reaction to Erika Christakis' email is supposedly a drive intended to make them safe in the face of this threat. But what exactly is it that they are supposed to feel so afraid of?

Ostensibly, it is the racism of their fellow students, especially the white ones, as that may be manifest in their choice of Halloween costumes, it appears. But what could that racism come down to?

Let us be realistic. There is no more racism among the white students at Yale than there was among their counterparts at Oberlin. How could there be? If you suppose that racism is an ideology that might have been transmitted to them from an older generation, you will not be able to find a ground for it. These students did not grow up in an atmosphere of racism, but of political correctness. Few, if any, of them has ever encountered an expression of racism from anyone who meant it. Their experience with the kinds of symbols thought to convey racism has strictly been as items to be wary of that they found out about in learning to do the PC dance. These are upper-class students who are at this Ivy League university because of its function as a way station on the mobility track. What benefit could they possibly gain from adopting a racist perspective? Is their status so precarious that they need someone to look down upon? These are serious matters. We have to be serious about them. If they felt the need to look down upon someone, they could pick the students at Cornell, or one of the other lower ranked schools of the Ivy League.

The racism that students A, B, and C feel themselves subjected to at Yale is entirely in their minds, and by this point we know it well. We see what it comes down to most clearly in the case of Student A, Michaela, who, charges Christakis with racism on the basis of the fact that he did not remember her name. She is one, but for Christakis, she is 1 in 500. The intolerability of his dealing with her in accordance with that is what she calls racism.

But what does this have to do with Halloween? Nothing, except that once the IAC recognized that seeing Halloween as a menace would provide a good venue to assert dominance, it was the responsibility of the whole Yale community to provide their assent. When Erika Christakis did not, as we know, hell broke loose; not because of what she said, but because she of what she did not say, which was, simply "Okay."

The issue here is who is going to be boss. At the most general level, it is which way of organizing society will prevail. On one side, we have the paternal function and objective self-consciousness. Its champion here was Nicholas Christakis, who spoke of the acceptance of universally binding rules of behavior. Others have rights, he said, not just you. A person has a wide range of obligations, which he must uphold, but of which we all should be cognizant. In order to maintain and develop social order we need to communicate with each other, which means we must have civility and grant others the right to disagree with us. His job is to work within and through these rules and create an intellectual space.

On the other side, we have student C, who says that his job is to ensure that she can be her pristine self. He must understand how she sees herself and on what terms she appreciates herself, as an absolute, and validate that. She claims this right to his services on the basis of her membership in an oppressed and marginalized race. His job is to ensure that any threats to her preferred way of seeing herself are condemned and eliminated. That is what she calls making a home for her. If he does not do that, that means he is a racist.

But in addition to the general issue there is the specific issue of the governance of Yale University. On one hand, we have the academic side, manifesting the central university function, as it has been defined since Plato's Academy. On the other, we have the IAC, a group that would traditionally have been thought of as being within the distinctly secondary function of student services, but which has, it appears, adopted the ambition of redefining the university though control of the ways in which students interact with and talk to one another. Their Mission Statement defines their role in the terms of identity politics:

> The Intercultural Affairs Council of Yale College strives to support an inclusive and diverse campus environment that: engages in community dialogue; promotes cultural awareness, respect and appreciation; and challenges bias on the basis of race and ethnicity, gender, religion, sexual orientation, disability, social class, or other distinction. (Intercultural Affairs Committee 2016)

When Student C says that Christakis function is to provide her with a home, it is their orientation to the university that she demands he accept.

But this home that she has in mind is a fantasy. It exists only in the mind and cannot be any place else. To turn the university into a home for her would make it unrecognizable in the terms with which we have thought of universities, redefining them in the way Ray Bradbury's novel *Fahrenheit 451* redefined fire departments. They would eschew objectivity and become zones of imaginary combat between fantasies of goodness and fantasies of evil.

At the most general level, the truth is that her way, given its profoundly narcissistic assumptions, makes social order impossible. We need not go farther than Hobbes to recognize this. Even if we forget about the dimension of fantasy, treating everyone's subjectivity as an absolute, even if we only limit ourselves to the oppressed and marginalized, and of course anyone can find a way in which they have been oppressed and marginalized, can only lead to the State of Nature and the war of each against each and all against all.

And indeed that can hardly be the end of it, either, since in these circumstances some, ultimately one, will rise to dominance. Her way leads inevitably and ineluctably to tyranny.

So where are we then? I say we are at Thermopylae. But Christakis, with all his virtues, is a doubtful Leonidas.

> "I have disappointed you and I'm really sorry," Nicholas Christakis told about 100 students gathered in his living room on Sunday for a meeting also attended by Jonathan Holloway, the dean of Yale College, and other university administrators. Christakis said his encounter on Thursday with students in the college's courtyard, in which numerous black women upbraided him for being inattentive to them, broke his heart, according to a voice recording of the conversation provided to The Washington Post.
>
> "I mean it just broke my heart," Christakis said. "I thought that I had some credibility with you, you know? I care so much about the same issues you care about. I've spent my life taking care of these issues of injustice, of poverty, of racism. I have the same beliefs that you do … I'm genuinely sorry, and to have disappointed you. I've disappointed myself." (Stanley-Becker 2015b)

And his faculty colleagues at Yale are no Spartans. An open letter supporting the Christakises was written by Douglas Stone, a professor of physics, calling for signatures among the active and emeritus faculty. Ultimately, about 90 signed it, out of over 4000.

On 6 November, in a closed-door meeting with minority students, Peter Salovey, President of Yale, apologized for the school's failure to make them feel safe. "We failed you," he said. (Stanley-Becker 2015a)

On 3 December, it was reported that Erika Christakis had decided not to teach at Yale University anymore. (Jackson 2015)

References

Christakis, Erika. 2015. Email from Erika Christakis: "Dressing Yourselves," Email to Silliman College (Yale) Students on Halloween Costumes. https://www.thefire.org/email-from-erika-christakis-dressing-yourselves-email-to-silliman-college-yale-students-on-halloween-costumes/.

Concerned Yale Students, Alumni, Family, Faculty, and Staff. 2015. Open Letter to Associate Master Christakis. http://downatyale.com/post.php?id=430.

Foundation for Individual Rights in Education. 2015. https://www.thefire.org/cases/protesters-at-yale-threaten-free-speech-demand-apologies-and-resignations-from-faculty-members-over-halloween-email/.

Friedersdorf, Conor. 2015. The New Intolerance of Student Activism. *The Atlantic*, November 9.

Intercultural Affairs Committee. 2015. Email from the Intercultural Affairs Committee. October 27. https://www.thefire.org/email-from-intercultural-affairs/.

———. 2016. Mission Statement. http://yalecollege.yale.edu/intercultural-affairs-council-iac#mission. Accessed 15 Jan 2016.

Jackson, Abby. 2015. Yale Lecturer Whose Email Ignited a Debate About Racism Has Decided Not to Teach There in the Future. *Business Insider*, December 3. http://www.businessinsider.com/yale-professor-erika-christakis-will-not-teach-next-year-due-to-racial-controversy-2015-12

Stanley-Becker, Isaac. 2015a. Yale's President Tells Minority Students: 'We failed you'. *Washington Post*, November 5.

———. 2015b. Hundreds March at Yale in Solidarity with Minority Students. *Washington Post*, November 9. http://www.businessinsider.com/yale-professor-erika-christakis-will-not-teach-next-year-due-to-racial-controversy-2015-12

Index

H.S. Schwartz, *Political Correctness and the Destruction of Social Order*, DOI 10.1007/978-3-319-39805-1

T

MIX
Papier aus verantwortungsvollen Quellen
Paper from responsible sources
FSC® C105338

Printed by Books on Demand, Germany